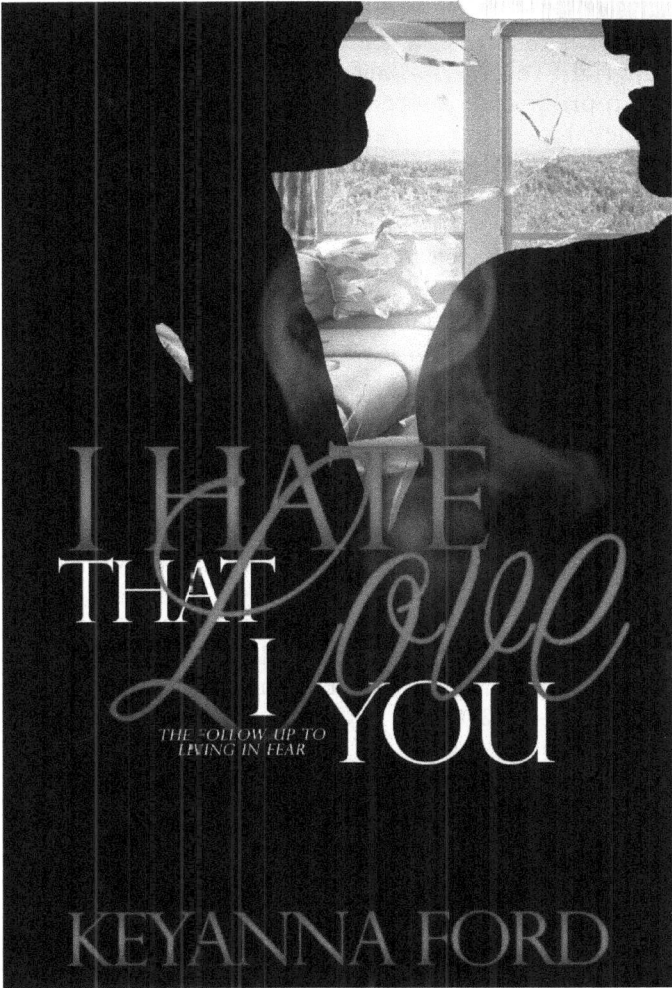

I HATE THAT I Love YOU

THE FOLLOW UP TO
LIVING IN FEAR

KEYANNA FORD

PUBLISHER'S NOTE:
This book is a work of fiction. Names, Characters, Places, and incidents either are products of
the author's imagination or are used fictitiously. Any resemblance to actual events or locales or
persons, living or dead, is pure and entirely coincidental.
Copyright © 2015 Keyanna Ford
All Rights Reserved, including the right of reproduction in whole or in part of any form.
ISBN: 978-0692403112

Library of Congress Catalog Card Number: in publication data.
I Hate that I Love You
Written by: Keyanna Ford
Edited by: David Good, The Editing One
Text Formation: Write On Promotions
Cover Design and Layout: TSP Creative Design
Printed in the United States of America

Dedication

I want to dedicate this book to every girl that has lost themselves in a man at one point in their life, we've all been there and unfortunately some of us never wake up.

Acknowledgements

I would like to thank all the people in my life who believed in my dream before I did. I wrote this book for fun just to see if I could and I remember getting to chapter 5 and putting it down. That was until my friends made me pick it back up and finish it because they believed in it that much. Without my friends there would have been no book. With that being said I have to thank Ebony Johnson and Katrice Woods for being the first to read my book. They were dedicated to it as much as me and having them there to talk about my character made it so much easier to finish my book.

I also want to thank Ciera Arnold and Tamika Harris for being my test readers once I finished. They must have read my book a thousand times and was still begging for more. The way they loved my book gave me enough confidence to put it out here.

I also want to thank my mom Patty Arnold who encouraged me to send my book in to have published. I was scared of being rejected until my mom convinced me and to my surprise, I actually got offered a few contracts. If it wasn't for her I probably would have never sent it in.

I also have to thank any and every one that had something to do with this book from the guy who inspired the story, he knows who he is so there's no need to name names to Amelia Eason for taking all my pictures for my website, promotions and back of the book.

I Hate That I Love You

Chapter 1

Mike

I couldn't believe Ace was in the room; he was supposed to be at camp, I thought as I banged on the door, trying to get in. Nobody answered. I heard Tia screaming through the door and I knew I had to do something. I went down to the front desk to get another key. I came back upstairs and when I got in the room, I saw Ace on top of Tia, choking her with one hand and punching her in the face with the other. I walked over and grabbed him off her. I was a little stronger than Ace, but I couldn't hold him long. I let him go and as soon as I did, he turned around and gave me a right hook, hitting me right in the middle of my jaw. I tried to grab his arm, but he hit me again in the same spot. I could feel the pain in my face. I didn't want to fight Ace, but I knew it was no use. I can't say I blame him. If I was him and just found out my best friend was sleeping with my woman, I would be mad too.

"So, you're fucking Tia?" he yelled and stood there, staring at me. I was about to answer, but then he turned around and walked toward the door. "I can't believe this shit!" he screamed as he walked out, shaking his head.

Ace

I couldn't believe Mike and Tia were fucking. My own fucking brother and the only other person I had in this world. I couldn't even lie, that shit hurt to have the only two people you have in the world sneak around behind your back. I wondered how long this had been going on and if he's been the guy all along. The PI said she was only hanging with him and he was buying her shit. The more I thought about it, the madder I got. I should just go back there and put a bullet in both of them, but I need to be smart about it. Trust me, they will pay for this, I thought as the elevator reached the main floor. I walked past the desk clerk and walked across the street to my car. I wanted to cry, but I'll be damned if I shed a tear for those scandalous bitches.

2

Tia

I saw Ace punch Mike in the face and that's when I started to get off the bed. I could barely see but I made it to the bathroom and locked the door. I walked over to the sink and saw my reflection in the mirror and cried. My lip was busted and my eyes were bloodshot red and swollen. He showed no mercy on me and it showed. I grabbed a towel, wet it and was about to clean my face when I heard somebody knocking on the door. I jumped, stopped moving my hand and looked at the door. I was scared to open it. I can't take anymore, I thought as I stood there, not making a sound.

"Tia, it's me," I heard Mike say from the other side.

I didn't want to see him either. I would never have been in this situation if he wasn't blackmailing me. Now I don't know what I'm going to do. "Go away! This is all your fault!"

"I'm sorry, but I needed to see you. Can you please open the door?"

"No! Leave me alone," I said and turned on the shower. I didn't want to deal with this anymore and I needed to clean myself up. I jumped in the shower, enjoying the hot water on my skin and drifted away from this madness I was in. I finally got out the shower, dried off and walked over to the sink. I stared in the mirror and my eyes were getting bigger by the second. I needed to find me some sunglasses

3

and fast. I combed my hair down, which made it look a little better, grabbed the towel, wrapped it around my body and walked out the bathroom. I was shocked when I saw Mike laying on the bed, flicking through the channels. "Why are you still here?" I said, walking over to him.

"I couldn't leave without making sure you were alright."

"I'm fine," I said, holding my head down. He walked over to me and lifted my face up by my chin.

"No, you're not. Your eyes are swollen."

"I know, but it'll be alright. I'm more concerned about Ace. Where did he go and what does he have planned?"

"Yeah, me too. He just stormed out."

"I'm going to get dressed and go home. If he's there, then I'll just have to deal with it."

"And what if he kills you?"

"Then he kills me. After all of this, I deserve it anyways," I said, putting my clothes back on.

"Nobody deserves to die." He walked over to me.

"I don't wanna talk about it, next subject." I patted him on the chest and walked away. I put on my shoes and caught a glimpse of my reflection. Every time I see myself I wanna cry. I hated the person I had become, and maybe Ace killing me wouldn't be so bad.

4

Mike

I wasn't leaving this room until I knew if Tia was alright or not. She had locked herself in the bathroom, so I had no choice but to wait. What I wasn't prepared to see was those two black eyes she had on her face. Ace had fucked her up and here she was about to go right back to him. "Why are you going there?" I said as I grabbed her keys.

"Because that's where I live. Plus, it's not like I can really run from him. I got myself in this mess and I'm going to accept all consequences."

"Maybe I should go with you."

She scrunched up her face and gave me this crazy look. "That's a joke, right? I'm already dead and now you're trying to make it happen faster. If you came with me, I wouldn't make it to the front door."

"I won't walk in the house with you."

"I know, because you won't make it through the front gate with me," she said, shaking her head. "Now give me my keys so I can go."

"I'm not giving you anything."

"I'm not really in the mood for this. I'll worry about me and you need to start worrying about yourself," she said and grabbed the keys out my hand. She walked toward the door and looked back. "I'll be alright," was the last thing she said before she walked out.

I just sat there, watching her leave. I knew she was in for hell if Ace was at that house. I wanted to go and save her because I knew Ace, and he was crazy. He's going to kill her, then come and kill me too. I had betrayed him and now he knew. I was supposed to be his brother, I thought as I sat on the bed with my back against the headboard, lighting a blunt. I had to think of my next move because I knew Ace wasn't going to just drop this. Maybe I could just move away and start fresh. Go to another city where nobody knows me and start over. That was better than dying, but I wanted to take Tia with me. I couldn't leave her with that monster. I have to go to my house to get a few things, then I'm going to go and get Tia, I thought as I finished the blunt, got up, and grabbed my keys.

Ace

I walked in the house and got upset instantly. *Were those bitches fucking in my house and in my bed,* I thought as I walked through. "Everything in this bitch has to go." I walked around the house, tossing shit on the floor. I tossed the pillows off the couch. "He probably hit it here," I said out loud to myself. "Hell, I did!" Then I went upstairs to *our* room. I opened the door and stood there, standing in the doorway, just looking at the bed. I still couldn't believe Mike would betray me like this. Yeah, Tia was foul, but Mike was my brother and he should have known better. I walked over to the bed and was about to pull the cover off, until I noticed a picture on the dresser.

I leaned over and picked it up. I noticed it was an ultrasound and a piece of paper for Tia. It was done a few days ago and on the paper was a note that said she was two-months pregnant. Two months ago, I thought. I was home then and I know for sure nobody else was hitting it, so I knew that had to be my baby. Plus I was putting it to her heavy; there was no way nobody else could be the father. Yeah, this is my baby, I thought as I continued to look at the ultrasound. This should have been one of the happiest days of my life. Instead, I had to find out like this; after I just found out the bitch was cheating. That shit just pissed me off even more. I wanted to kill both of them, but I couldn't kill this bitch now, especially if she's pregnant with my baby. "Mike on the other hand doesn't get a temporary pass; that bitch has to go," I said, walking out the bedroom, down the stairs, and out the door.

Tia

I was driving home trying to think about what I was going to say to Ace when I got there. I knew he would probably be there waiting, or maybe even putting me out. Hell, I didn't know what to expect, but what I did know was that I was just going to tell the truth from the beginning, I'm going to tell it all. From how I came on to him to the blackmail, though I'm not telling him about the first pregnancy. Some stuff is just better left unsaid, I thought as I pulled up to the gate. I put the code in and watched the gates open. The more they opened, the harder I started to breathe. I pulled up in front of our house and killed the engine. I looked around but I didn't see a car anywhere. I didn't know what Ace was driving, but I didn't see anything out of the ordinary. This made me feel a little better and my breathing slowed down a little. I got out the car and walked the pathway to the door.

I gripped the door knob. My hand was shaking so bad I couldn't get the key in the lock. I took a deep breath and tried to relax. I finally got myself together, opened the door, and walked into a trashed house. The pictures that used to be on the wall were now on the floor. The cushions from the couch were tossed everywhere. He'd thrown the lawn chairs in the pool and destroyed all the food. "I can't believe this shit," I said, walking toward the stairs. *Yeah, Ace may not be here now, but he has definitely been here,* I thought as I walked up the stairs. I got to the top and walked to our room. I was shocked to see nothing was wrong with it. It was totally intact; no clothes thrown on the floor, no mirrors busted or nothing. I walked over to the bed and sat down. "What a day," I said, lying down on the bed. All I wanted to do was go to sleep. I laid there with my eyes open, staring at the dresser, and that's when I noticed the ultrasound picture was gone. I looked behind the dresser and around it, but I couldn't find it. *Ace must have seen it. Does he think it's Mike's baby? Where did he go?* So many things were running through my mind I didn't know what to do. I laid back down and grabbed my pillow, holding it tight in my arms as I rolled over to the other side and cried myself to sleep. *How did this happen to me?* My life was supposed to be different.

Ace

Somebody has to pay, I thought as I walked out the door and got in my car. I got on the freeway and headed to Mike's house. I knew he had to come home eventually, and I was going to wait here until he did. The question was what I was going to do with him when he came. He was my brother and I still loved him, despite what happened, but he couldn't be trusted. Everybody I have ever loved had betrayed me in some way, and now I'm really alone, except for my baby Tia's about to have, I thought, looking down at the ultrasound.

It seemed like forever before Mike was finally pulling up. I was in his room looking out of the window, waiting on him. I didn't have to worry about getting in because we had keys to each other's homes. Tameka wasn't here and hopefully she won't be coming home soon. I would hate for her to get in the middle of this; she's alright in my book. I heard the door open and footsteps coming up the stairs. I stood behind the door and waited for Mike to come in the room. He came in a few seconds later, turned on the light and went straight for the closest. He grabbed a suitcase and started packing. *What the fuck, this bitch is running. Where is he going?* He had his back turned to me and I snuck up behind him "Why you do it man?" He turned around and looked shocked.

"Man…it just…happened."

"What you mean it just happened?" I asked, walking closer to him. "You knew how I felt about her and this is what you do behind my back? You're supposed to be my brother."

"I'm sorry, man, but you weren't treating her right," he said, looking away. When he said that, I could feel my blood heating up and I lost control. Who the fuck does he think he is? I wasn't treating her right? What the fuck he trying to say, he can treat my bitch better than me? I walked all the way in his face.

"I wasn't treating her right?" I said low, looking him in the eyes.

"Naw man—" he started to reply, but I was done talking. I dropped him to the floor and pulled out my pistol. I gave him a few knocks to the head and he was out. I tried to pick him up, but this nigga was heavy. I tied him up and called my homeboy, Brian, to help me. I was about to hang up, when I heard somebody say "Hello?"

"I need your help," I said through the receiver. Brian was both mine and Mike's childhood friend, but him and I had a tighter bond, and I'm counting on him to help me execute my plan.

"Where you at? Is something wrong? I thought you were supposed to be at camp."

"I'm over Mike's house, I'll fill you in when you get here." I didn't want to tell him too much because I wanted him to come.

Brian finally got here about an hour later, and I led him upstairs to Mike's body. I had to hit him a few times to keep him conscious, so he had a few bruises.

"Man! What the fuck is going on in here?"

"I found out this nigga was fucking my woman."

"So you tied him up and beat him?" he said with a puzzled look on his face. "Man, this shit is crazy; I'm leaving," he said, walking toward the door.

"Wait! I know this is crazy, but they betrayed me. He knew I loved her and he slept with her anyway."

"So you're going to kill your best friend over a girl?"

"Not just over a girl, but over the person I love, and this bitch betrayed me. Sat in my face every day and was fucking my girl behind my back. I love that man like a brother and he crossed me. This is what happens when you cross me." I walked over to Mike and beat him in the face with the butt of the gun again. I turned around, walked over to Brian and looked him in his eyes, "So are you going to help me or should I just sit you next to him and kill y'all both?"

"Kill us both? Nigga if you don't get out of my face. I'm going to help you because you're my boy, but don't you ever threaten me again. Now, what are you going to do with him?"

"Cremate him," I said, walking back over to Mike. I didn't need to say anymore because Brian's uncle owned a crematory and he already knew what I needed from him. We carried him downstairs. I pulled the car up on the lawn, in front of the door. We threw Mike in the backseat, good thing it was one something in the morning and people weren't out. I got in the driver seat and pulled out, following Brian.

Chapter 2

Tia

I woke up in the middle of the night to go to the bathroom, and when I got off the bed, I thought I saw someone sitting in the chair, but it was dark. It looked like a shadow, so I just dropped it. Plus, both my eyes were swollen. When I came out, I was more alert and there he was in all black. I didn't know if I should get back in bed or turn around and hide in the bathroom.

"Don't be scared. If I wanted to hurt you, it would have already happened. I've been watching you sleep for a minute," he said, leaning back in his chair.

I just stood there frozen. I didn't know what to say. I know the conversation about Mike is coming, and it's not like I could deny the shit if I wanted to.

"So you're pregnant?' he said in a low tone, breaking my train of thought.

"What!" I was startled by the question.

"Are you pregnant?" he asked again, never raising his voice. This time, he leaned up in the chair and turned his head toward me.

"I am and before you ask, yes it's yours."

"How many months?"

"Two," I said, walking over to the bed, sitting on the edge.

"When did you find out?"

"Wednesday."

"Have you fucked him since you've known you had my baby in you?"

"No."

"How long have you been fucking him?" he questioned.

"A few months," I said, looking at him, waiting for his reaction.

"Were you fucking him at the Christmas party?"

"Yes and no."

"What the fuck you mean yes and no?" he said, raising his voice.

"Umm...I was messing with him before the Christmas party, but by the time the party came around, I hadn't seen him in minute."

"Was Tameka telling the truth? Were you guys about to kiss?"

"He was trying to kiss me, but I wasn't going to, so I walked back in the kitchen." I figured he already knew I was fucking him, so I might as well tell the truth from here on out and put it all on the floor.

"When did you start, and why? And don't say you don't know cuz I ain't trying to hear that."

"We started right after the birth control incident. He was there to comfort me when you weren't."

"When I wasn't?"

"I mean…when…" I started to stutter.

"Just stop it, Tia, before you piss me off more. So, tell me the story. I wanna know where it happened, who came on to who and if y'all did more than just have sex. Did y'all date? Do you love that nigga?" he said, looking at me and getting angry.

"No, I don't love him." I don't know if I was lying or not because I do like Mike and he's different from Ace, but I know I love Ace and that's who I want to be with.

"You better not," he said, mean mugging me. "Well I'm listening," he said, leaning back in the chair, waiting to hear my story.

I took a deep breath and started talking.

Ace

Tia was sitting on the bed, telling me about this affair she's been having. I couldn't help but get upset when I heard her talking about how her and Mike have been sleeping together for almost a year. She said she came on to him because she was hurt and he was there to comfort her. They never fucked in our bed—let her tell it—and she said they broke it off a few months ago when Mike started blackmailing her because he said he loved her.

I just sat there staring at her, not knowing what to say. I can't believe all this shit that has been going on behind my back. I knew some funny shit was going on, and to think, I was talking to Mike about the bullshit this whole time. Thinking about the conversations we would have and how he would always try to get the suspicion out of my head just made me madder. It was all because he was the other guy.

"Did y'all use condoms?"

"Yeah."

"Okay," I said and got up. I wanted to put my hands on Tia so bad, but I couldn't because she was pregnant, so I had to get up out of there. I had heard enough. I wasn't feeling neither one of them and I don't know which one hurt me more.

Tia

I couldn't dare tell Ace I was fucking Mike raw. I wanted to ask him to stay, but I knew I just needed to leave him alone and let him come around when he was ready. I fucked up and now I have to deal with the consequences. Ace was being real cool about this and it was scaring the fuck out of me. I thought I would be dead by now for sure, but instead, he's walking around here like nothing major happened. I wanted to call Mike, but I knew better. I got in bed, pulled the covers over my head and closed my eyes.

I woke up the next morning and Ace still wasn't there. I walked downstairs and stood at the bottom step, looking around. *I guess I should clean up.* I walked off the step and started picking stuff up off the ground and putting the cushions back on the couch. I had picked up everything and was headed upstairs, when I heard the door opening. I stopped and turned around and saw Ace coming through the door. I turned around and kept walking up the stairs. I really didn't want to see anyone right now, including Ace. I felt so ugly with these two black eyes and busted lip.

"Where you going?" he yelled.

I came back down the stairs a little. "To take a shower," I said in a low tone.

"Come here."

I started walking down the stairs with my head down. I made it to where he was standing and stood looking at his chest.

"I could kill you right now," he said and walked past me and up the stairs.

Ace

I felt a little bad for what I did to Tia, especially when I walked in the house and saw her face. I wanted to be nice to her, but I couldn't, and I was mad at myself for still liking this bitch. I called her over to look at her face, but all I could see was her fucking Mike, so I had to walk away. I couldn't even look at her without wanting to put my hands on her.

"Come take your shower," I said, continuing to walk up the stairs. I could see her just standing there, frozen. I stood at the top of the stairs for a minute, waiting on her. "Are you coming?"

"Yeah, I'm coming," she said, jumping as if I scared her.

"Why are you jumping?"

"I didn't know you were standing there," she said, starting to walk up the stairs.

I turned around and walked in the room. She came walking in a few minutes after. "Hurry up and get dressed. I want to take you somewhere."

"I'm not going anywhere with my face looking like this." She said turned around and looked at me like I was crazy.

"Don't worry about that because where we're going, no one is going to be concerned with how you look."

"Where we going?" she said, putting her hands on her hip. Even with her face all messed up, she was still trying to be cute and sassy. A part of me wanted to take her and be her doctor, but another part of me wanted to just shove her head into a wall. I hated the fact that I still loved her, and it was pissing me off.

"Don't worry about that, just get ready," I said, sitting on the bed. I have to let her know that this kind of behavior is not acceptable to me and somebody is going to pay.

Tia

I wonder what Ace has up his sleeve, I thought as I got in the shower. I took my time letting the jets massage my body, before I finally got out. I looked at my hands and they had pruned up. I dried off and went to the sink to put on my baby oil and brush my teeth. My lip was still swollen, so it was a little hard to brush. I tried the best I could to cover my black eyes, and I did an okay job. They still looked swollen, but I couldn't see the blackness. I walked out the bathroom and found Ace stretched out on the bed, asleep. He looked so handsome and I just wanted to go over and cuddle with him so bad, but I thought against it and headed toward the closet.

I found something to wear and got dressed while he slept the whole time. When I was done, I sat on the bed next to him and rubbed the side of his face. He didn't move, so I started rubbing on his arms and the back of his neck. I leaned down, kissed him on the cheek and whispered in his ear, "I love you and I'm so sorry. I hope you can forgive me one day." I know things weren't perfect between us, but I love this man and because of me, things will never be the same again. I am so angry with myself for getting in that situation, and I wish I could take it all back.

"Don't put your lips on me again," he said without opening his eyes.

"I can't kiss you anymore?" I said with an attitude.

"Were you kissing on Mike with those lips?" he said, opening his eyes to look at me.

"No."

"You're fucking lying. Get out my face, now. I can't even look at you. I swear if you weren't pregnant..." he said, shaking his head.

What he said hurt my feelings and I could feel tears forming in my eyes. "I'm sorry," I said and got off the bed. "I'll be downstairs. I'm ready when you are," I said, walking out the door.

"Yeah! You do that."

Ace

I wanted to be nice to Tia and her rubbing me felt good, but I just couldn't give in to that like a sucker. Every time I try to be nice to her, all I see is her and Mike. I don't know if I'm going to ever get over this, I thought as I closed my eyes. I had to get my mind right before I took care of business. I'm going to take Tia with me so she can learn her lesson. I hate snakes and backstabbers, and today is the day the grass gets cut and the snakes get exposed. But right now, I need some more rest. I've been going all night and I'm exhausted.

20

Tia

I went downstairs, sat on the couch, and turned on the TV. I watched *Law and Order* until Ace decided he wanted to come downstairs. I must have watched three episodes by the time he finally came down, talking about he was ready. I grabbed my coat out of the downstairs closet. I wonder where he's taking me, I thought while putting it on. "Where are we going?"

"You'll see," he said, walking out the door. I walked out behind him and got in the car. We drove until we got downtown. "You hungry?" he said, pulling up in front of a pizza joint.

"I'm not going in there," I said, pushing my glasses up, holding my head down, and covering my face with my hand.

"Calm down, I'm going in. I already ordered it anyways," he said, getting out the car, laughing. "You were about to have a heart attack if you had to get out the car." He went and got the pizza, got in the car and handed it to me, then he drove off. He pulled up to a parking spot a few blocks over that overlooked the water, and turned off the engine. We sat there in silence, eating and looking out the window. Ace hadn't really talked to me since the whole Mike thing came out, and I was really getting tired of it. We had been in this car for an hour now and he hadn't looked my way, except to ask about the food.

"Do you hate me now?" I said, breaking the silence.

He turned his head and looked at me. "I don't know how I feel. I wanna hate you, but my heart won't let me."

"I just wanted to say that I'm really sorry. I know I fucked up, but I wasn't in the right mind frame and I never meant to hurt you. I just wanted some love and you weren't giving it to me. Do you think you could ever forgive me?"

He didn't say anything for about ten minutes, then he finally said, "Maybe one day, but not today." He started up the car while saying, "Y'all really hurt my feelings. I can't believe y'all would do that to me behind my back. The only two people I thought I had left."

I just sat back in my seat and didn't say another word. I felt like shit. We drove for about another hour. I started getting a little nervous when we started passing all these trees as we drove up a hill. It looked like we were driving through the forest before we finally stopped in front of this warehouse. "What are we doing here?" I said, turning my head to look at him. I couldn't really see anything because it was dark, but I saw smoke coming from the roof.

"Don't worry about it," he said, getting out. "Get out."

What the hell are we doing here? This looks like the kind of place you take people when you want them to disappear, I thought, getting out the car. When I got out, I could smell an odor in the air, but I didn't recognize the smell. I followed Ace to the front of the building. He walked in the door and I stood on the step for a minute, hesitant to go in. I couldn't shake this feeling that something bad was going to happen, and something inside of me was telling me not to go in this door.

"Come on!" he said, knocking me out of my train of thought.

I walked in the door and followed Ace around a hallway. It was dark and I couldn't see anything. We walked through another set of doors and when I walked in, I could see someone sitting in the chair. When he turned on the light, I noticed he was not only sitting in the chair, but was also tied to the chair. I got scared and started to shake when I noticed he was bloody and had a pillowcase on his head. It looked like a morgue in there, but fire was burning from the wall. He walked over to the person and pulled the pillowcase off and my heart stopped when I saw who it was.

Chapter 3
Ace

I made Tia come with me so she could see Mike. It was time they learned their lesson, plus I wasn't just going to let it die. She's lucky she was having my baby or she would be in the seat next to him. I pulled off the pillowcase, looking at Tia the whole time because I wanted to see her reaction when she saw who it was. She jumped and I could see her starting to breathe harder. "What's wrong?" I asked smiling.

"What's this?" she asked, pointing to Mike. "Why is he tied to the chair like that?"

"I don't know, Tia. You tell me?"

"What you mean, you tell me? You're the one calling all the shots, now I hope you're not about to do something stupid," she said, shaking her head.

"Something stupid," I said looking at her, confused. "Like what? Fuck my man's best friend or fuck my best friend's girl? I don't know, Tia, you tell me."

"So because we had sex you have to kill Mike?"

"Damn right! I trusted y'all and y'all betrayed me. Do you know how much that shit hurt? Huh, Tia? Having the only two people you have in the world betray you with each other," I said with tears in my eyes. I refused to let them go and let these bitches see me cry.

"I'm sorry, Ace, and I'm sure if you let Mike speak he would say he's sorry, too."

"You know what? You're right, why not let Mike speak," I said, taking the towel out his mouth.

"Man, I'm sorry, it just happened," he said as soon as I took it out.

"What the fuck you mean it just happened? Shit like this don't just happen. Y'all had no right fucking each other, and then when I was talking to you about the other guy you knew the whole time you were the other fucking guy. You are supposed to be my brother and look out for my girl if anything, not fuck her."

"Man, she came on to me. I tried to walk away but…I…I couldn't," he said, hanging his head.

"I bet you couldn't," I said looking at her in disgust. *This little slut was the one coming on to him. I want to fuck her up so bad, but I know it will have to wait, standing over there trying to look all fucking innocent and shit. That bitch is a slut,* I thought looking at her standing by the door in the same spot with her hands folded across her chest.

I let them talk some more, trying to plead their case but it was no use; my mind was made up and they both were wrong. "Okay, I'm done listening to this shit. Tia, sit down in that chair behind you and you shut the fuck up! Both of y'all betrayed me and that's the end of it," I yelled, putting the towel back in his mouth.

I had already preheated the chamber when I left here the first time to go get Tia so everything was ready to go. I walked over to Tia and handcuffed her to the pipes so she couldn't run out, then I walked back over to Mike and punched him in the face repeatedly with the butt of my gun that I pulled out the back of my pants. I beat him until he passed out, and then I stuffed him in a box sitting next to him on the left. Tia was screaming the whole time and I wanted to go shut her up, but instead I just ignored her and continued what I was doing.

I already had the box on a lift so I was able to pull it over to the burning chamber. I walked over, opened the door and pushed the box in. As I pushed it in I let a single tear fall from my eye as I said goodbye to my brother. I wiped my face, turned around and walked over to Tia who was screaming and crying uncontrollably.

"Oh my gosh, oh my gosh," she kept screaming over and over.

"Shut up," I said, walking over to her and that's when I heard someone else screaming and I

26

knew it was Mike; he woke up and now he was being burned alive. I un-cuffed Tia and she started hitting me. I grabbed both her arms and put them behind her back and whispered in her ear, "This is what happens to people who betray me. You got lucky you're having my baby, so you better count your blessings."

"Fuck you, Ace," she said, trying to get away. "You just burned him alive, don't you hear him screaming?" she said, breaking down crying. "Why did you do that? That wasn't necessary!" she screamed.

"Yes, it was. He can't be the only person walking around here that's ran up in my baby momma."

"So if I fuck somebody else you're going to kill him, too?" she said, looking up from the floor.

"Yup, but don't worry about that because you won't get the opportunity to fuck anybody else, you slut. I'm going to make sure I keep my eye on you from now on, and then after you have my baby you can try it if you want, but you can be right here next to Mike, and I'll be taking care of my baby alone. You better not tell anybody because good luck on proving anything."

"I don't belong to you. I'm not your property, you know," she said between tears.

"That's where you're wrong. Now get the fuck up and let's go!" I yelled. She got up and stood there for a minute, looking at me. "You're a monster," she said, walking out the room to stand in the hallway. I came out after her and started walking toward the exit, and we headed out the door and got in the car. We didn't say anything the whole ride home. When I pulled up she got out the car, ran in the house, and up the stairs.

Tia

I lay in the bed, crying. I couldn't believe Ace had just done that to Mike. I started shaking and throwing up. I was so scared and shook up I didn't know what to do. I was going home. I don't care what I look like, I had to get out of here. He couldn't stay away from camp forever, so when he goes back I was leaving. I couldn't roll up, so I went to sleep to try to forget about the day, but I don't think that would ever happen. *I just saw my boyfriend kill his best friend because we were fucking, what the fuck have I gotten myself into?* I thought as I closed my eyes and passed out.

I woke up the next morning in an empty bed. On the low I kinda missed Ace and wish we could have sex and cuddle. *I still love him through everything that's happened, and I wish this hadn't of gone down the way it did.* I got up and got in the shower. I put on some sweats and headed downstairs. I checked the whole house and nobody was there. *Where did Ace go?* I thought as I went back upstairs to get my phone. I called him and nobody answered so I called a cab to the airport. The cab said they would be about 45 minutes so I decided to pack a few things since I had time. Finally, my phone rang and the cab was outside, but when I went to leave somebody greeted me at the door. He was a tall black heavyset man who looked like he played no games.

"Who are you? And what are you doing here?" I said walking past him to get in my cab, but I looked around and I didn't see a cab anywhere.

"Oh, I sent that cab about its business."

"What! Nobody told you to do that," I said looking at him like he was stupid. "Who are you? And what are you doing here?" I yelled.

"I'm here to make sure you don't do anything stupid like try to run away," he said, taking my bag out of my hand and walking it back in the house.

"Ace sent you here, great! So now I have a babysitter," I said plopping down on the couch. "Where did Ace go?"

"He had to go back to camp."

"So am I not allowed to go anywhere?" I said crossing my arms in front of my chest and rolling my eyes.

"Not unless I'm with you."

"You're with me," I said turning up my nose. "I don't need a damn chaperon."

"Well, somebody thinks you do."

I got off the couch and went upstairs. *Ace has gone too far. I couldn't believe I was now a prisoner in my own house and I have to have a chaperon everywhere I go. I need to get away from this relationship, but now I'm starting to think it's impossible.* I needed to talk to someone to clear my head, so I picked up the phone and dialed Neek.

"Hey, girl," she said, answering on the third ring.

"Hey, what you up to?"

"Nothing really, just been going to school. I'm taking summer classes this semester. What about you?"

"I decided to take this summer off. You know I needed a break, but fall is coming in about a month."

"Yeah, so how are you and Ace doing?"

"We're doing good. I just found out I'm pregnant" I said, smiling over the phone.

"Congratulations!"

"Thank you, I haven't told anyone yet."

"Does Ace know?"

"Yeah, he knows, but I haven't told anybody outside of him."

"When are you going to tell people?"

"Soon, I just have to wrap my head around the fact that I'm pregnant before I tell everybody else." *Plus I have to let my face heal because I know everybody is going to want to see me when I let them know.*

"Well, I'm happy for you and I can't wait to meet my god baby," she said all excited.

"Me either, but enough about me. What's new with you?" I asked. *I want to tell her so bad about Mike and the situation I am in right now, but I am too scared. I have to get away before I let someone know.*

"Nothing really, still doing me. You know."

"Yeah, I do. Did you get into the sorority?"

"Yeah, I got in. It's nice to be a part of something bigger than you. I love it." *I was a little jealous listening to Neek talk about college. That was supposed to be me. I was supposed to be a part of a sorority having the time of my life, enjoying the parties, and building lifelong friendship. I hate how my life is turning out and I know it's time to do something different.*

"That's great. I see you're really doing everything we planned on doing."

"Yeah, college life is just how we imagined it would be. I just wish I had you here with me."

"Me too," I said sadly.

"What's wrong?"

"Nothing, sometimes I just wonder if I made the right choice."

"Are you having doubts about your decision?"

"Naw," I said trying to play it off. "I went after love and that's what I got. I just wanted to experience the college life also, and I'm a little sad I'm missing it."

"You'll be okay, and as long as you're happy that's all that matters."

"Yeah, you're right," I said, forcing a smile. "So tell me about some of your sorors. Do you like them all?"

"They're pretty cool. I live in the house and we haven't had any problem, and I've been spending a lot of time with this girl named Katrice."

"Katrice" I repeated remember that was Ace's old girlfriends name. "Not the girl that used to date Ace? And why are you hanging out with her?" I asked a little annoyed. *Neek is supposed to be my best friend, so why and the fuck would she be hanging out with a girl she knows used to date my man. I would never do that to her and I can't believe she'd be associating with the enemy.*

"At first I didn't know she used to date him, but then I found out and I decided to stay friends with her to try to get the scoop."

"The scoop on what, Neek? And I hope you don't be sitting up gossiping about me with that bitch," I said, mad.

"On Ace. Maybe she knows something about him that we didn't know, and hell no, I didn't tell her anything about you, but she did tell me something."

"And what was that?"

"That she was planning on paying Ace back for what he did to her, and she was going to make something happened to him, but she didn't know where he lived."

"And did you tell her?"

"No, I didn't. Who do you think I am? I know you love that nigga and I wouldn't help anybody try to harm him even if he is putting the hands on you."

"I'm just making sure. Stop hanging out with her. I don't need my friends hanging with the enemy. What did Ace do to her anyways?"

"Let her tell it he left her for you, but according to everybody else they were just fucking and she read to into it. I'll stop hanging with her if it makes you feel some type of way, but I wouldn't betray you like that."

"That's good to know. She should have known her position and played it better and I wouldn't have been able to come in a take her man," I said, and we both started laughing. "It was nice talking to you, but I have to go now. I'll call you later," I said and hung up the phone.

What kind of shit is that? My best friend befriending a girl who she knows my man used to date? I'm not going to lie, that right there made me question our friendship and think twice about the things I tell her. Maybe our time apart has strained our friendship and she's becoming loyal to someone else. All I know is I'm going to put some distance between us and try my best to get out of this relationship for the sake of me and my unborn child.

Shynika

I got off the phone with Tia and I could sense a little tension. I guess she got mad because I told her I was friends with Katrice, but if she only knew the real reason behind the friendship. I thought about telling her more details about what Katrice was planning, but when she got mad just because I was talking to her I knew she wasn't going to believe me. I told her I didn't have anything to do with the plan, but I couldn't tell her the truth. I'm just going to never bring it up again and leave Katrice alone; being her friend is not worth losing my sister over plus I don't need to get in the middle of Tia's relationship. I love her and we've been through way too much for me to betray her with someone I just met.

I walked out of my room and into the living room where a few of the other sorors were. I live in a sorority house, so there's always someone around. "Hey y'all," I said as I sat on the couch on side of Prize. Prize was becoming one of my best friends here. I could talk to her about anything, and I wanted to get her advice on this Tia situation. "Can I talk to you alone?" I leaned over and whispered in her ear.

"Of course, is everything alright?"

"Yeah, things are good. I'm just in the middle of a situation and I need some advice"

"You wanna talk here? Or we can go to lunch later."

"I would rather go to lunch so we could be alone," I whispered back to her.

"Okay, I just have to throw some clothes on and run a few errands, and then we can head out," she said, getting off the couch and heading up the stairs.

Prize was one of the realest people I've ever met and I know she would give me the truth about what I should do. She would also tell me if I was wrong for even considering the idea of befriending Katrice in the first place. I hadn't told anybody about the plan and I didn't need everybody in our business. So that's why we're going out because when living in a house with ten females it's the only way to get privacy.

Chapter 4
Ace

I walked in the room and Tia was sleeping. I wanted to get in the bed with her but I decided against it. I wasn't sure what I wanted to do with her yet. I loved and hated her at the same time. I called a few people to try to get someone to watch Tia before I went back to camp. After what I did to Mike I didn't trust Tia to stay here by herself, who knows what she would do especially since I killed him. I sat down in the chair and put my head in my hand. I still couldn't believe I killed him. Mike was the only family I had left and now he's gone and on top of that I did it. I didn't know how to feel and my emotions were everywhere. After making a few phone calls I finally got someone to watch Tia then I headed back to camp. I still had to play my role and get back to my daily activities, no matter what happens in my personal life.

Tia

For the past few weeks I'd been in my bed crying myself to sleep. I thought about Mike all the time and I was so irritated by this guy watching me nonstop. I hated it. I tried to sneak away a few times but it was no use, I couldn't ditch him. One night when I thought he was sleeping I tried to sneak out the door, but when I was halfway out he woke up and asked me where I was going. I thought about making a run for it but I knew it was no use. I wanted to leave this house and go back to Kalamazoo, but Sean won't let me go anywhere. I just hope things change once Ace comes back from camp next week because I don't know how much more of this I can take before I snap. I got out of bed and took a shower. I had to get ready for school. Today was the first day and this was one of the few things in my life that I considered normal and had the luxury of doing.

I attended the University of Illinois and planned on enrolling in their nursing program. I was putting on my clothes when somebody knocked on the door. It could only be Sean since it's only us two in the house. "Yeah?" I yelled through the door.

"You almost ready?'

Sean had been taking me everywhere and school was no exception, but I didn't know why he was up here checking on me. His job was to drive me around and make sure I didn't run away. I walked over to the door and flung it open. "Yeah, why? You checking on me now?"

"Naw, I was just making sure you were getting ready. I didn't hear any movement."

"Whatever, I just have to put on my shoes and grab my purse and then I'm coming". I rolled my eyes, closed the door, grabbed my shoes out of the closet then sat on the edge of the bed and put them on. I grabbed my purse off the chair and headed down the stairs. When I got to the last step I saw Sean sitting on the couch, rolling a blunt. I wished I could hit that right now, but I'm pregnant and Ace would kill me if I dared. *Plus I wanna give my baby a fair shot,* I thought looking down, rubbing my stomach. "I'm ready," I said, walking toward the door.

"Hold up, I'm almost done," he said licking the last piece of paper over and lighting the blunt to dry it off. "Alright, now I'm ready," he said, standing up and putting the blunt behind his ear.

"You do know that's illegal," I said, leading the way out the door.

"Well, there's no police around and if you're not going to tell on me, shut up," he said jokingly.

I laughed and got in the backseat of the truck; if I had to have a chauffeur I was going to play the part. "To the University!" I said when he got in and closed the door. I leaned up and said in his ear, "We need to get you a hat so you can look like a real chauffeur." I sat back and started laughing.

"I'm not trying to be a real chauffeur."

"I can't tell. I'm going to get you one today. Now let's get to school."

"I'm not your servant."

"I know, your Ace's because if it was up to me you would be gone."

38

He turned around in his seat to face me. "Listen, I'm nobody's servant. I'm here on a favor and that's it. If you hadn't of been creeping you wouldn't have this problem." He turned back around in his seat, took the blunt from behind his ear, lit it and pulled off. I couldn't believe what he had just said, but he was right. I brought all of this on myself and only I can fix it. I didn't say a word the rest of the ride because I was a little embarrassed. I went to class and found me a seat in the front while Sean sat in the back and watched me, I guess. I felt like a prisoner in my own body and I didn't have any privacy. *One more week of this*, I thought as I sat down and got my supplies out. *I just hope Ace is nice to me when he comes home.* I smiled and opened my notebook up to the first page and prepared to take notes.

Ace

I've been getting weekly updates on Tia and she hasn't been doing anything but she hasn't had the opportunity to either. When he first got there Sean said she had a cab waiting and was about to leave. She probably thought she was going home. I wish I could have seen the look on her face when she saw him for the first time. I bet she was mad as hell. I haven't talked to her since I left. I'm really not sure what to say to her; they hurt me and I can't trust her, but she's having my baby and I love her. I'm confused and the person I would usually go to is no more. I think I'm more fucked up over that then I am over Tia. Why couldn't it have been somebody else? That's all I think but that still would have been a problem because I don't want anybody else to have her. Especially now since she's having my baby, I'll be damned if she goes anywhere with my child.

We'll find out if I can handle being around her soon since I go home tomorrow. It was good being away from her theses few weeks but I needed to deal with this situation and get it over with one way or the other. I walked in my room and headed toward the shower. A few of us was going out to hit the town before we went back home. I got dressed and headed to meet up with the rest of the fellas. We were going to a bar downtown.

When we got to the bar it was nice in there, but nothing to special. There were three floors to it and every floor played a different genre of music. The hiphop music was on the third floor so that was where we made our way too. We got on the elevator, made it to the third floor and when I stepped off this shorty on the dance floor caught my eye. She was with her girls standing by the bar, not really dancing but more so swaying to the music a little and she was gorgeous. I stood there for a minute, taking in the scenery when she must have felt my eyes because she turned around and gave me a smile, and her teeth were perfect.

"Aye, look at shorty right there in the white dress. She bad," I leaned over and whispered in one of my fella's ears.

"Yeah, she is but what about Tia? She bad, too," he said reminding me that I had a girl at home, but I could care less. I had never stepped out on Tia before but right now it's fuck her. "I'll be back!" I yelled over the music and started walking away. There was something about shorty that had me wanting to know more, I'm not sure what it is but I wasn't passing up an opportunity to get to know her. "How you doing, Miss Lady?" I asked, walking up behind her.

She turned around with her face turnt up, but when she saw it was me she smiled and said, "I'm fine, how you doing?"

"I'm doing much better now that I've seen you."

She started laughing. "I bet that's what you say to all the ladies."

"Not really, but I would really love to buy you a drink."

"I'm already drinking," she said, holding up her glass. "How about I come find you when I need another one?" she said taking a sip from her drink.

"How about a dance instead?" I said walking closer to her. She smelled good and I wanted to sweep her off her feet and take her right there. I don't know if it was her smooth chocolate skin or the way her ass looked in this dress, but baby girl had a body and a face to match.

"I don't really dance," she said turning back around facing her girls.

"Damn, if I didn't know any better I would think you weren't feeling me," I whispered in her ear.

"I don't know you to be feeling you or not feeling you, but what I do know is I don't go to the club looking for a man nor do I find men at the club."

"I can respect that, but I'm not your normal guy that you meet at the club. My guys and I were just here celebrating," I said, pointing over to my crew.

"That's nice, but that doesn't change anything."

"Can I at least have your name? If you give me that I swear I will leave you alone."

She turned back around to face me and smiled. She extended her hand and said, "Sky...Sky Taylor."

"Anthony Ealy," I said shaking her hand. "Nice to meet you, Sky." I let go of her hand and walked away. I don't care what I had to do but I was going to get a date with Sky. I went back to the table, thinking about her smile and her scent. Sky Taylor was all I thought about for the rest of the night as I sat back and watched her and her girls enjoy themselves.

The next morning I headed home. It was the moment of truth, I was going to see Tia but Sky was on my mind heavy. I pulled up to the house. I sat in the driveway for a minute smoking a blunt because I wasn't sure what was about to happen. I chilled there for about 30 minute, and then I finally got out. When I entered the house I saw Sean sitting on the couch watching TV. "What's up boy?" I said, walking over to him giving him some dap.

"Shit, chillin."

"How was babysitting duties?"

"Boring as fuck. Next time you get somebody else to do this bullshit."

"I told you I didn't have anybody else to do it, plus what about all those times I looked out for you growing up?"

"That's why I'm here, but I'm not doing this shit no more. Next time get Mike to do it, after all that is your brother."

Just the thought of Mike made me mad but I had to play it cool. "Man, I haven't really seen Mike since he moved out. I guess he don't need a nigga anymore."

"You know how it is when you're over there playing house."

"Yeah, I know and that's why I ain't tripping."

"I haven't heard from him since I got here either. I called him a few times, but he never hit me back."

Don't take it personal, he won't be calling anybody back I thought laughing to myself. "He's probably just busy. I'm sure he'll call," I said. *Sorry, but Mike won't be heard from ever again.* "Where's Tia?" I said changing the subject.

"She's upstairs."

I grabbed my bags and headed up the stairs to my room. When I walked in Tia was sitting in the bed, flicking through the channels. "Hey," she said when she saw me walk through the door. She was three months now and her stomach wasn't really showing yet, but you could see it on her face.

"Hey," I said walking over to the closet. I put my bags in there and went and sat next to her in the bed. A part of me wanted to kiss her, but another part wanted to slap her.

"How was camp?"

"It was good. How's school going? You like your classes?" I asked, making small talk. No matter what I still love this girl and that's not going to change.

"Yeah, it's alright" she said, getting on her knees and putting her arms around my neck. "I'm missed you." I missed her, but every time I look at her all I see is her fucking Mike.

"Get your hands off me" I said moving her arms.

Tia

I couldn't believe Ace was acting like that. *When is he going to get over this?* I thought as I sat with my back against the headboard, staring at him. "Are you going to be mad at me forever?"

"I don't know."

"What do you mean, I don't know?"

"Like I just said, Tia, I don't know. But why don't you tell me, how long should it take me to get over it?" he said, getting closer to me.

"As long as you need," I said a little nervous. "I just thought we were trying to get over this, but you seem like you're not letting it go."

"I'm sorry if it's not that easy to let go of the fact that my girl was fucking my brother. To be honest with you, I don't know if I could ever let this go. The only reason you're still in front of me right now is because you're carrying my baby." He said getting off the bed, he walked in the bathroom and closed the door. I could hear him turn on the shower as I leaned up against the headboard. Ace had just hurt my feelings and I wanted to cry, but I couldn't because I had no one to blame but myself.

Tameka

I'd been calling and calling Mike, but he hasn't answered or called me back in a few weeks. The last time I heard from him he sent some text talking about he was going out of town because his mom had gotten sick. His mom lived in Texas and I'd never met her, but just because he was with his mom didn't mean he couldn't answer the phone. I was starting to get worried because this isn't like him. *I wonder if Ace heard from him*, I thought as I picked up my phone and started to dial his number. *He got back from camp today and I just need to make sure Mike is alright. Maybe he can give me his mom's number.* The phone started ringing and Ace picked up on the fourth ring.

"What's up, Tameka?"

"Nothing much. How've you been?"

"I'm good. What's got you calling my phone?" he said, getting to the point.

"I was seeing if you've heard from Mike. I've been calling him for weeks now and his phone keeps going straight to voicemail."

"Naw, I just got back from camp. I'll call and leave a message, then let you know if he calls me back. When was the last time someone seen him?"

"He sent me a text saying he was going to see him mom's in Texas."

"Alright, I'll call her and see if he's there."

"Can I have her number? I wanna call myself," I said. *I can't believe this bitch hasn't called me in almost a month.*

"Naw, I don't give out people's numbers and especially if you're calling down there starting drama. I'll tell him to call you. Alright?"

"Alright." He hung up the phone. I sat on the couch, watching my phone, waiting on Mike to call me so I could cuss him out.

Ace

I couldn't give Tameka Mike's mom's number because she would know something was wrong when he wasn't there. There was no need in me calling her, so I would have to think of something to tell Tameka. I could just ignore her calls, but then she would suspect I was up to something because I've never done that before. *I could tell her he was there but didn't want to talk to her and I wasn't getting in the middle of it. Yeah thats what I'm going to do but what if she goes down there or finds the number and he's not there? Naw, I'm not going to say that, that's too easy to prove. I'm just going to say no one answered.* I picked up the phone and called her back.

"Hello?" she said on the second ring.

"Alright, I called his mom and nobody answered. I'll try again later and let you know."

"Alright, I'm worried about him and if I don't talk to him soon I'm going to call the police."

"I'm sure he'll turn up. Let's give it a few more days before we get the police involved," I said, trying to buy some time to figure out my next move.

"Yeah, you're probably right. I'll wait a few days, but if I don't hear from him by the end of the week I'm putting out a missing person's report."

"I'll call tomorrow and let you know," I said and hung up the phone.

"Why did you just lie to her?" Tia asked when I got off the phone.

"Why you all in my business? I don't think I was talking to you," I said, walking to the dresser to grab something to throw on. I just got home and couldn't even enjoy one day before I had to deal with bullshit. I had to do something about this Mike situation because sooner or later Tameka was going to go to the police and I had to make sure I have an air-tight alibi.

"You don't have to keep being so mean to me." She got off the bed walked out of the room. I was glad she was gone because I didn't feel like dealing with her right now. I already had enough on my plate, plus the season was about to start. I threw on some sweats, rolled up, and laid across the bed. I need a nice long nap I thought as I dozed off.

Tia

I don't know who Ace thinks he's talking to, but I'm not going to keep taking this disrespect. If this is how he wants to treat me then I'm going to leave, whether he likes it or not. I walked out of the room because I felt myself getting mad and I didn't want to go there with him right now. I went downstairs and called Neek. I needed to vent to someone and she was the only friend I had.

"Hey girl," she said right before I was about to hang up.

"Dang, what took you so long?"

"I couldn't find my phone, calm down."

"I was just saying. I was about to hang up."

"But you didn't. Now did you call me to talk about why I took so long to answer or did you want something?" she said jokingly.

"No you didn't," I said through giggles. "I called to vent about this asshole."

"What he do now?" Neek doesn't know anything about what went down between the three of us and I wanted to tell her everything, but I couldn't risk her opening her mouth. After all the last time I talked to her she did tell me that she was friends with Katrice. So I always tell her the bare minimum to get my point across so she could give me some advice.

"Being an ass. He got back from camp today and he's acting like he doesn't even wanna touch me. I'm tired of this relationship and I'm ready for this to be over. I don't care if I'm pregnant. Women take care of babies all the time by themselves. Hell, my mom raised two kids on her own."

"Did you talk to Ace about it? Why are you done now? Like, did something happen?"

"No, nothing happened," I said, lying through the phone. "But things aren't the same. It's like he's a whole different person."

"I kept telling you that nigga was too good to be true."

"I know but now is not the time for I told you so's. I want out and he won't let me leave."

"What you mean, he won't *let* you leave?"

"Well he told me that I couldn't leave him because I was pregnant with his baby and he wanted to raise his baby no matter what."

"That's a good thing but you guys don't have to be together in order to raise a child together."

"That's what I told him but what I think the real reason is, is that he don't want anybody else to have me. He was my first and he wants to be my only." *Which is why Mike had to die. Ace didn't want somebody else walking around this earth saying that they fucked me. This dude is too territorial for me,* I thought.

"You know what? You're probably right. That's what you get for putting it on him like that."

"Who you telling?" I said and we both started laughing.

"But on some real-ish, if you really wanna leave, just leave. Don't think about the consequences and just go. If you need me to come help, you know I will."

50

"Thanks, girl, and you're right. I need to stop making excuses and just leave. I'll be alright, after all I have my family."

"That's right."

"Alright, girl, thanks for letting me vent, but I have to go. I'll call you later. Love you," I said and hung up the phone. Neek was right. I needed to just leave if that's what I really wanted to do and that's what I plan on doing. I walked up stairs and went in the room prepared to tell Ace that I was leaving, but when I got to the room Ace was asleep. I decided to just grab a few things and get out of there because all that shit can be replaced and I didn't know when I would get this opportunity again. I grabbed a bag a filled it with pictures and other irreplaceable items and walked downstairs. Ace's flunky was gone. I grabbed his car keys and left. I jumped in the car and didn't look back. I was debating on if I wanted to drive there or to the airport to catch a flight. I decided to drive. I needed the time alone to think about my next move. *When Ace finds out I'm gone he's going to come looking for me and I know the first place he's going to go was my mom's house, but I have to go there because I have nowhere else to go.*

Ace

I woke up from my nap and looked at the clock on the nightstand; it was 11 o'clock. I had been asleep for almost six hours. I turned over and Tia wasn't there. She was probably still mad at me and was downstairs. I got up and went to the bathroom and then headed downstairs, but when I got to the bottom steps I didn't see her on the couch. I walked in the kitchen and she wasn't there either. I walked around the whole downstairs and even went to the backyard, but I didn't see her. I opened the door and noticed my car was gone. I immediately picked up the phone and started calling her number, but it went straight to voicemail. I went back upstairs, sat on the bed and dialed her number a few more times, but it was no use because it kept going straight to voicemail. I got up and looked in the closet and all of her stuff was still there. I checked the drawers and nothing was missing out of there either, so she didn't go far. I sat back on the bed and rolled a blunt. *She probably just ran to the store or something*, I thought as I lit it and flicked through the channels.

It was getting later and later and Tia was still nowhere to be found. *Where the hell is this girl at? It's one in the morning now and she still hasn't answered a call. I hope nothing happened to her since she's carrying my baby.* I decided to just lay back down and deal with it in the morning, if she's not here then I'll call the police and make sure she's alright. I tried to go back to sleep, but I couldn't. Not knowing where Tia was at was driving me crazy. I got on Facebook and tried to inbox her but her name wouldn't come up. What the fuck was really going on? I looked up Neek and asked her if she seen Tia.

It said she was active so it shouldn't take her that long to respond. She responded in a few minute telling me that she hadn't seen her but she talked to her today. I asked her if she said she was going anywhere and she said no. Then I asked if she could call her for me and make sure she's alright and let me know.

Shynika

I picked up my phone and dialed Tia's number. I thought she might have been sleeping, but she answered the phone on the third ring and it sounded like she was wide awake.

"Hello?"

"Hey, girl, where you at? And why is Ace in my inbox looking for you?"

"Probably because I left today while he was sleeping and came back home. I didn't tell him anything and I blocked him from calling my phone. Why, what he say?"

"Nothing, just asked me if I seen you and if you were alright. He seemed worried."

"Yeah, I'm sure he is," she said sarcastically.

"So, you really left?"

"Yeah, I drove here today."

"And you don't think he'll find you at your mom's house?"

"I'm sure he will, but where else was I supposed to go? Plus, I'm not hiding from him."

"So it's cool if I let him know where you're at?"

"Naw, let him figure that out by himself. That nigga killed Mike and I'm done with him. Let that nigga worry." I had said Ace killed Mike without even thinking about it and now the cat was out the bag.

"What do you mean he killed Mike?" I asked in shock.

"It's a long story but Mike is dead, Ace did it, and I need to get as far away from him as possible."

"Then you need to go somewhere else. Come to campus. He won't be able to get you here and you need to go to the police and turn Ace in."

"I'm not calling the police on Ace, Are you crazy? No matter what that's my baby's father and you better not tell anybody either. I'll see you tomorrow, I can't go anywhere else tonight. I'm tired and the only place I wanna go is to sleep."

"I'm not going to tell anybody but you should. I don't understand why you love that nigga so much but that's none of my business. Now get some sleep, I'll come see you tomorrow and we can come back together. I'm not telling Ace shit. Actually I'm about to block him and go to sleep.

"You make sure to get some rest too."

"I will and you can tell me the whole story tomorrow."

"Alright, girl, I love you."

"Love you, too." I hung up the phone from Tia and I couldn't believe what she just said. Ace had killed Mike. *I knew that nigga was crazy*, I thought as I blocked him from my Facebook and logged off.

Ace

I was sitting in the bed, waiting for Neek to message me back. I felt like I was waiting forever so I decided to see what was up, but when I searched her name nothing came up. Her picture was also gone from the conversation we were just having and I couldn't send her another message. This bitch had just blocked me and that could only mean that she had talked to Tia. That's when I knew nothing had happened to that bitch but that she had left. I was so fucking mad I threw my phone across the room. I told that little bitch she couldn't go anywhere until my baby was born. So she wants to sneak out while I'm sleeping? She didn't go anywhere but back to Kalamazoo to her mom's house. I laid down. I tried to get some sleep, but I couldn't. All I could think about was the fact that Tia left and she's the only one that's knows about what happened to Mike. *I need to get her back here and now*, I thought as I got up and put on some clothes. *I'm going to get her and I don't care if I have to kidnap her*, I thought as I grabbed my keys and walked out the door.

Chapter 5
Tia

I heard something pounding in my sleep and I thought I was tripping. I opened my eyes and tried to adjust to the dark when I heard it again. *Boom! Boom!* I heard it again. I got up and walked out the room, down the hallway. Who the hell was pounding at my door? I looked at my watch and it was 4 in the morning. I swear somebody better have died I thought as I reached the door. "Who is it?" I yelled but nobody answered, instead they started knocking again, but harder this time. "Who is it?" I yelled again. I tried to look out the peep hole, but it was pitch dark and I saw nothing. I started to just walk away, but something told me to open the door and when I did I was in for the shock of my life. "What are you doing here?" I said nervously.

"I came to see you," he said, walking through the door. "You just left and didn't say goodbye. I was worried about you."

"Oh, so now you're worried about me?" I said, closing the door.

"I'm always worried about you and my baby."

"Well, we're fine as you can see so you can leave now," I said folding my arms across my chest.

"I just drove 2 ½ hours to see you and this is the hospitality you show me?" he walking past me, inviting himself in. He sat on the couch, pulled out a blunt, lit it, and just sat there staring at me.

"Well come on in," I said sarcastically. "And what are you looking at?" I said. getting a little freaked out.

"Come here and sit down," he said, patting the cushion seat next to him. I reluctantly walked over to the couch and sat down. Ace was being too calm about me leaving and I didn't know if I should be scared or not. We sat there in silence for a minute before he finally spoke. "Why did you leave?" he said low.

"Because you hate me," I said not wanting to face him. *The truth is I still love him and I regret fucking with Mike, but at the same time I am terrified of the nigga, too.*

"I don't hate you. Truth is I'm not sure how I feel about you. On one hand I love you, but on the other you disgust me."

"So why do you want me around? I know you want a relationship with your baby and I won't stop you from that. I also won't tell anybody about what happened with Mike." *I lied because I had already told Neek.* "At the end of the day I love you and you are my baby's father, but I can't live like a prisoner," I said with tears running down my face.

"Who's fault is that? I need you to go and get your stuff so we can leave," he said in a low tone. "And I'm not going to tell you twice."

"I'm not leaving," I said, looking at him like he was crazy.

"This shit is not up for discussion. Now go get your shit so we can go. You are leaving and I don't care if I have to pick you up and drag you out. I'm tired of talking about it. Now come on before I get mad."

"You're going to have to get mad because I'm not leaving! I refuse to raise my baby in that type of environment. I don't know why you want me to come back anyways. All you want to do is lock me up and treat me like shit. Fuck that, I'm not going back." He just sat there smoking the rest of his blunt. Not saying one word.

Ace

I don't know who Tia thought she was talking to, but I wasn't in the mood to deal with her shit. She was leaving and that was that. I got up and stood over her. "I'm going to give you one more chance, now come on."

"I'm not going anyw..." she tried to say before I picked her up off the couch and threw her over my shoulder. I walked out the door and threw her into the passenger seat. "Don't try to run because if I have to chase you I'm going to beat your ass, pregnant or not," I said before I slammed the door.

I walked to the driver side, got in and drove off. We jumped on the highway and drove all the way to Chicago in silence. That was fine by me because I didn't have much to say to her anyways. Actually I really wanted to beat her ass. We pulled up to the house and I got out. I walked up to the door and Tia was still sitting in the car. "Get out!" I yelled at her. This bitch was working my last fucking nerves. "It's already 7 in the morning."

"I'm not going in there," she said, shaking her head. I walked back to the car and opened her door.

"Why are you being so damn difficult?"

"Why did you just fucking kidnap me?" she said, cocking her head to the side.

"I rescued you. You ran away, remember? Now are you going to get out the car or am I going to have to carry you?"

"Carry me," she said with a smirk on her face. I picked her up and carried her to the door. She wrapped her arms around my neck and I'm not going to lie, that shit did feel good. I wanted to just take her in the house and make love to her right now, but I couldn't. A part of me just couldn't let what she did go.

"I love you," she whispered in my ear as I opened the door, took her upstairs and laid her in the bed. I just looked at her, turned around, and walked out. I was having mixed feelings about her and I didn't feel like being around her. I left the room, went downstairs and started playing the game. I had to figure out what I wanted to do with Tia because I couldn't keep holding her in the house. I would either have to forgive her or kill her because I'll be damned if I let somebody else have her, but I have six months to figure that out. Maybe when the baby comes it might make it a little easier for me to forgive her.

Shynika

I rolled my blunt and sat in the bed, I was glad that Tia was finally about to get out of that situation. She was too smart for that and I would hate for her to loose herself in a man. The only bad thing was she's pregnant so no matter what she's going to have to deal with that nigga for the rest of her life. *I'm going to ride up there and get her tomorrow, so Ace won't be able to find her.* I went to sleep thinking about the craziness going on in my friend's life and how I didn't know anything about it. Had I been so consumed in my own life that I hadn't been there for my friend? I felt bad because Tia had always been there for me and not to mention what happened to Mike. I wanted to jump on the highway right now, but I needed some rest.

I woke up the next morning around 10 and got ready to get on the highway. I got in the shower, rolled up, ate breakfast and got prepared to take this drive. Kalamazoo wasn't but a few hours away, but I still hated driving on the highway. I was going to take one of my new friends, but I thought it would better to go alone; Tia probably needed a friend and I didn't want her to feel like I wasn't one anymore by bringing someone else. I got on the highway and made it to her house around 1, but when I got there nobody answered the door. I noticed a car in the driveway and I figured it had to be the car that Tia was driving because it had never been there before. I started calling her phone, but it was going straight to voicemail. I had to have called her over 20 times and nothing changed. *Could something be wrong?* I thought as I got back in my car. I was going to go to my mom's house and come back and check on Tia later. Maybe she was just sleeping. After all she has been through a lot lately.

I drove around the corner to my house and sat outside. I haven't been here in over a year. After I got out the hospital I went to school and have been staying there the majority of the time. I also haven't seen my mom since I got out. I wonder what she's been up to, probably the same shit she's been doing since as long as I could remember. I really didn't want to go in there because there was no telling what it looked like, but I had nowhere else to go to wait on Tia. I haven't talked to Jerome since I started college and I didn't want to start now. I finally got out the car and walked up to the door. I stood there for a few minutes before I put my key in and opened it. I was surprised by what I saw. The place was actually clean without me being there and not only that but it was decorated and smelled good. I had to close the door and look at the address because my mom hadn't had the place looking and smelling like this since before she got on the shit. Our house used to always smell like cinnamon and my mom always kept it clean until she started using drugs than I had to take over. I kept the house clean when I was here, but not as clean as her and I never burned the cinnamon candles because it reminded me of what life used to be.

I walked back in the house and went to the bathroom. Then I walked all through the house and ended up in the kitchen. I looked in the fridge not expecting to see much, but to my surprise it was a house full of food. *What the hell was going on?* I thought as I grabbed a juice and went to my room. I couldn't believe it in here and if I didn't know any better I would think my mom was back to her old self, but I won't get my hopes up. When I was little I used to pray that my mom would get better and kick her habit, but it never happened. I would beg her to get better, but it would never happen. Every once in a while she would clean her act up a little and I would get my mom back, but that wouldn't last long and she would go right back to the drugs after a few months. After she slipped back the fourth or fifth time I stopped getting my hopes up. I haven't seen my mom clean and sober since I was in the 9th grade. I thought about the last time my mom kicked the habit and I smiled, thinking about how happy we were. I love my mom and I wish she could stay clean, but I learned a long time ago that she thought drugs were more important than me. I rolled a blunt, smoked, and then took a nap. *When I wake up I'm going to go back over to Tia's house. She should be up by then*, I thought as I dozed off.

Ciera

When I got to my house I noticed a car parked in the driveway. I didn't know who that could have been since I've cut off all my friends and I just got back to the city about a month ago. I walked in and noticed a purse sitting on the kitchen counter and I knew that car had to belong to no one but my daughter. I walked to her room and opened the door. I saw her sleeping. I wanted to run over there and wake her up, but she looked so peaceful so I decided to leave her asleep and make dinner for when she woke up. *I haven't seen Neek in over a year and I've been trying to get right so I can be the mom she needs.*

I was going to make my baby her favorite meal: taco pie which is a taco in pie crust. This has been her favorite since she was a kid and today was all about making her happy. I started browning the meat and baking the pie crust so it could cook a little: you don't want it to cook all the way because after you put the meat and cheese in there you have to cook it again to melt the cheese. I finished cooking the pie and headed to my room to get cleaned up a little. I needed to take a shower and get comfortable. I lit a candle, got in the shower and stood there enjoying the hot water on my skin. I was nervous about seeing Neek. I'd always let her down and I didn't want to this time.

Shynika

I woke up from my nap and heard the shower running. It could only be my mom in there because nobody else had a key to the house. I walked in the kitchen and saw a taco pie sitting on the stove. She had just made that because that wasn't there before I went to sleep. I walked over the stove smiling because I love taco pie and my mom knew it. I cut a piece out and it was still warm. I put some sour cream on top and sat down in the living room. I was about to go check on Tia, but I wanted to see my mom first. I hadn't seen my mom in forever and it seemed like things were starting to change around here. I heard the shower go off and I sat back on the couch, watching the door like a hawk.

I felt like I was staring at the door forever before she finally came out, and when she did I couldn't believe what I saw. My mom looked good. She was healthy and I could tell she hadn't been using drugs lately and I couldn't help but run over to her and give her a big bear hug. "Hey, Mom, how've you been?" I said still hugging her.

64

"I'm fine, sweetie, but I can't breathe."

"Oh! I'm sorry," I said, letting her go. "It's just I haven't seen you in forever and you just look so...good," I said backing up looking at her. I felt like I was seeing her for the first time and I wanted to examine everything about her.

"Thank you, and yes we have a lot to talk about. So much has changed in my life since you've been in the hospital."

"Wait! You knew I was in the hospital?" I said in shock. She never came to see me and I just assumed she didn't know, but now she told me she did. Why didn't she come and visit me was my question.

"Yeah, Tia told me."

"So, why didn't you come and visit me?" I said with an attitude.

"We can talk about all of that in a minute but I need to throw some clothes on then I'll break it all down to you. I just came out here to grab something, I didn't know you were up," she said, holding her towel.

"Alright," I said reluctantly then went back and sat on the couch. *I still can't believe my mom knew this whole time that I was in the hospital and never came and seen me. And why didn't Tia tell me she saw my mom and told her?* I picked up my phone and dialed Tia's number again, but I still didn't get an answer. I couldn't wait to go over there and see her in a minute because we have lots to talk about.

Tia

I laid in the bed crying. I was sick of being a hostage. He took my phone so now I couldn't even talk to anyone. I knew Neek was probably looking for me and I needed to let her know I was alright. Ace was overreacting and I shouldn't have to live like this. I wanted to smoke so bad, but I couldn't. I closed my eyes and went to sleep, thinking about my next move. *I have to get out of here and since I just ran away Ace is going to be watching me like a hawk, but if I got away once I can get away again, but next time I just have to be smarter about it and have a plan.*

I woke up to go to the bathroom and I noticed it was 5 in the evening. I knew Neek was probably worried by now. I had to figure out a way to make contact with someone. I was just glad I didn't see my mom when I was there because that's one less person I had to worry about worrying. *The only person that knew I was in Kalamazoo was Neek, but then again I was only there for a few hours before I was rudely scooped up, but I'm still going to have to call my mom because she's going to wonder about the car in her driveway, or what if Neek goes over there asking about me?*

I got up and took a long bath. I didn't want to go downstairs and see Ace because I didn't want to deal with him and I really wanted to stay as far away from him as possible. *I don't know why he won't just let me leave. What's the point of keeping me here if he doesn't love me and all he wants to do is hold me hostage? Ace doesn't touch me or sleep in the same bed as me anymore. It's like he doesn't want me, but he still doesn't want anybody to have me and that shit is crazy.* I got out of the tub, put on some clothes and headed downstairs. I needed to use the phone to let someone know I was alright. I reached the bottom step and Ace was on the couch knocked out. His phone was on the table so I picked it up and dialed Neek's number. She picked up on the first ring.

"Hello?"

"Hey, girl, it's me." I said low.

"Girl, I've called you a hundred times and came by your house. What's wrong with your phone? And why you calling me private?"

Tameka

I was going through all the drawers when I finally found something that had his mom's address. I knew her name was Dawn Simpson and I found a letter she mailed to him that had his birth certificate in it. I knew this was her and I decided it was time to go and pay him a visit. Something was wrong and I didn't know exactly what it was, but this wasn't like Mike to leave and never call even if his mom was sick. I packed my bag and headed to the car. It was going to be a long ride from Chicago to Houston. I decided to go to the airport and see what type of flights they had, but they were all booked and the earliest I could fly out would be tomorrow night. I looked at my phone. It was 4 o'clock. Then I googled how long it took to drive to Houston which was 16 hours and something, so I decided to book the flight since I would still get there earlier than me driving and leaving today. I went back home. I couldn't sit down and my mind was racing. I was anxious to see Mike in a few hours, but I didn't know what to expect since I haven't talked to him in about a month. I grabbed a blunt and rolled up. I needed to relax a little. I watched TV until I passed out.

I woke up the next morning and decided to spend the day pampering myself. *I had to kill time before my flight tonight at 7, so I might as well go get my nails and hair done. I don't know, maybe even go and do a little shopping*, I thought holding my nails out in front of my face. "Yeah, I could definitely use a manicure," I said out loud. I got off the bed and threw on some clothes. The first thing I was going to do was call my hair stylist. She probably had a full house, but she usually fits me in when I was in Chicago, since I'd been going to her for almost a year now every Friday and sometimes Wednesday. I was one of her best customers so I knew she'd squeeze me in even though it was Thursday which was one of her busiest days. I dialed her number

"Hello," she said on the fifth ring.

"Hey girl, I need you today."

"I don't know about today, Tameka. I got a packed house."

"Come on, pleeeease, you can't squeeze me in?" I was trying to plead with her.

"What're you talking about getting?"

"I just need a flat iron," I said with a smile. "I have a fight at 7 and I have to make sure I'm right before I go see my man."

"You have a flight at 7? So that means you have to be at the airport at 6?"

"Yeah, that's why I'm calling you now. I was hoping you could squeeze me in now or in the next few minutes because I have other stuff to do. I'll pay double." She was quite on the phone for a minute and I could tell she was contemplating what I said about paying double. *I don't care what nobody says, people would do anything if the price is right.*

"Let me check my schedule. I might can get you in since you're willing to pay double and all," she said, giggling through the phone. "I can squeeze you in about an hour."

"Alright," I said looking at the clock on the nightstand; it was 11 am. "But I'm going to need to get right in and I don't want to sit under the dryer."

"Alright, miss picky, I'll see you in an hour."

"Alright," I said and hung up. There was no use in going to get my nails done yet because there was no way I could get a pedicure and manicure in under an hour, plus I had to drive. I decided to lounge around the house some more before it was time to go to my appointment. When I got to the shop I got right in the chair like I requested. I was in and out of there within an hour and a half, and then I was on to getting my nails done. I walked in the shop and there were a few people in there; I decided to wait because I liked the way one of the workers did my nails and I didn't let anyone but her do them. I didn't have enough time to go to the mall due to the fact that it took me longer than I thought with my nails. It was 4:30 and I only had enough time to go and get dressed and head to the airport.

I took my time getting dressed. I hadn't seen Mike in almost a month and I had to make sure I was snatched when I saw him. I put on my lip gloss and did one last twirl in the mirror "Yeah, I am cute," I said as I grabbed my clutch and headed out the door. I arrived to the airport at 6:05, it took a half hour to make it through security and the closer I got to the departure time the more nervous I became. It was time to board the plane and I could feel my stomach getting tight and I wanted to turn back, but I was next to get on the plane. I hated that I had to go through these lengths to see Mike, but I needed answers. I found my seat and took a deep breath. *It is time to face the music*, I thought as I closed my eyes and prepared for takeoff.

Ace

I fell asleep on the couch and when I woke up the whole day was gone. I got up and walked up stairs, and when I went in the room Tia was in the bed sleeping. I walked over to her and stood there for a minute, I was debating on whether or not I wanted to touch her and despite what I was feeling I still loved her. I rubbed her cheek, bent down, and kissed it. I squeezed in bed behind her and started rubbing her stomach. I hadn't cuddled with her since I found out she was pregnant. Her stomach was so smooth and hard; I wanted to lay here and rub it all day. I started kissing her on the neck. I moved my hands up her stomach to her titties and started playing with her nipples. I was squeezing them lightly between my thumb and index finger until they started to harden, then I went under the covers and took the one I was just playing with in my mouth while playing with the other one. I was taking turns flicking her nipple with my tongue and sucking it. I moved my mouth to the other nipple and slid my hand down her body until I got to the top of her pajama shorts. I put my hand in her shorts and started rubbing her pussy. Even though I hadn't touched her in months she still kept it neat down there and I loved it.

I put my index finger in her hole and her spot was dripping. I could feel my pipe getting hard. I opened her legs so I could get better access to it and I started playing with her spot like I was on recess. I took my index finger in and out of her hole several times then started playing with her ring. Her pussy was so wet and I wanted to get in there so bad. I took my clothes off then her shorts. I climbed on top of her and stuck my pipe in her hole. Her hole was so tight that it probably would have hurt if it wasn't so wet. I started grinding in her spot when I heard her start to moan. I looked down, saw her eyes open then felt her hips moving. *I forgot how good her pussy was*, I thought as I started pounding harder. I started sucking on her titties and playing with her clit at the same time. I lifted her legs up so I could get better access to her wet spot and I went in. I started teasing her, putting my pipe deep in her stomach then pulling it out slow. I watched my pipe go in and out of her hole and she begged me to stop playing with her.

"Ace, please give it to me!" she screamed, pulling my hips closer to her.

"You want this?" I said still teasing her. "I wanna hear you say it."

"Yes, I want it."

"Turn over then." She turned over and got on all four. I lined my pipe up with her hole and held one ass cheek in each hand. My pipe was so hard that it was pointing straight forward. I lifted up her cheeks and slid my pipe in. I went as deep as I could and started pounding in her spot deeper and deeper until I felt her body start to shake. I was about to get mine, but I couldn't. The image of Mike fucking her popped into my head and I couldn't help but think of him fucking her like this. I slid out of her. "Was that nigga fucking you like this?" I asked as I sat on the edge of the bed.

"What?" she said in shock.

"Were you fucking that nigga the way you be fucking me?" I asked again.

"No, Ace, I wasn't," she said, crawling over to me. "I can't fuck anybody the way I fuck you because I love only you."

"Were you sucking that nigga's dick?"

"Hell, naw, that was for you and you only."

"I thought that pussy was for me and me only, too."

"It is, but I made a mistake. Ace, I'm sorry I did that to you and I'll do anything to make it up. I love you and I wish things could be back the way they were, but I know it's going to take you some time, but like I said before you can't hold this against me for the rest of my life and if you do then you need to let me move on with it." She kissed me on the cheek and whispered in my ear, "I love you and that will never change."

"I'm not going to lie, Tia. I love you too, but you hurt me and I don't know if I can ever trust you again. Trust is everything in a relationship and without it you have nothing. How am I supposed to trust you? If you would cheat on me with my brother, who knows what else you would do. I've tried to forgive you because you're carrying my baby, but I don't know if I can."

"I understand, but all I ask you to do is think about it and take it one day at a time," she said as she grabbed my pipe in her hand and started rubbing it. "I know it's going to take time, but I think we can get past this," she said, putting the tip of my pipe in her mouth. She started sucking on the head like it was a sucker and I couldn't do anything but enjoy it. I leaned my head back and let her do her thing. She started sucking my pipe faster, putting the whole thing in her mouth. She played with the slit of it with her tongue, and then sucked and played with my balls until I came. She got up and ran to the bathroom to spit and I knew she was brushing her teeth, something she always does after giving head.

Tameka

I arrived in Texas a little after nine. I had a rental waiting for me at Avis along with a hotel room. I got a room right by the airport and went there first to put my bag up. I touched up my makeup and headed to the car. I put the address in the GPS and it said I was a little over an hour away. I took a deep breath and started up the car and headed over to Mike's mom's house. The whole time I was driving all I could think about was what I was going to say to Mike. I was replaying the conversation I was going to have with him in my head over a thousand times. I played out ever scenario I thought could happen until I arrived at the address that was on the paper. I parked in front of it and cut my lights. I took a few deep breathes, got out the car, and walked up the sidewalk to the door. *The house was dark and it didn't look like anyone was home, but I'll be damned if I came all this way for nothing,* I thought as I reached the door. I knocked on the door and stood there. I must have stood there for about a minute but nobody came to the door. I looked at my phone and it was close to midnight. Maybe they were sleeping, but I didn't care. There was a car in the driveway and I wasn't leaving until someone opened this door. I knocked harder then started to beat on the door until I finally saw a light come on upstairs. This was the moment of truth; somebody was coming to the door and I was starting to breathe heavier and heavier with every second that passed. I was thinking about running away. *But fuck that, I needed answers,* I thought as I heard someone say, "Who is it?"

"Tameka!" I yelled threw the door.

"I'm sorry," I heard someone say then heard the locks unlocking. The door opened and there was a tall slim lady on the other side. She was pretty and looked like a female version of Mike; there was no mistaken that this was his momma and she looked fine to me.

Tia

"This is Ace's phone, that's why," I whispered to Neek.

"What do you mean, Ace?" she said startled. "What are you doing with him? And where are you anyways?"

"I'm in Chicago. He came and got me in the middle of the night and made me come. He also took my phone and is holding me hostage." *I was tired of living this life and I want out*, I thought as I told Neek everything.

"Girl, I'm going to call the police."

"No…no, don't do that, that's not necessary. Just come down here and get me," I said not waiting to get the police involved. After all I did still love him.

"Okay, I'm on my way."

"No, we need a plan. You can't just come down here trying to be super save a hoe. I told you he already killed somebody."

"That's why we need to go to the police."

"I said no police. I'm not going that route."

"Okay, then what's the plan?"

"It's five o'clock now, so why don't you get my brother and a few more people, and you guys come and get me. You guys should be here by 9 or 10 since it might take an hour or so to get everybody together. I can last until then," I said trying not to kill everything Ace has by calling the police.

"Alright, I'll get a few people together and we'll be there no later then 10. You better be ready and Ace better not put up a fight."

76

"Alright" I said and hung up the phone. I erased my call from the call log and put Ace's phone back in its spot, then I went back upstairs, set my alarm clock to 8 and went back to sleep. Sleep was the fastest way to kill time, plus I was tired. I got comfortable and pulled my pillow in my arms and closed my eyes. When I woke up Ace was inside of me giving me something I hadn't had in a minute and it was feeling damn good.

£££

I got done brushing my teeth and I just stood there looking in the mirror. I was happy that Ace had touched me and even though he was still mad about the whole Mike thing we were making progress, but I was still leaving tonight no matter what. One good moment doesn't substitute for all the bullshit I'd been through these past few months. I finished up in the bathroom and walked out. I got back on the bed and scooted behind Ace who was lying down. "Do you still love me?' I asked. *I needed to know if he still love me even though I was leaving. I didn't want us to end hating each other even if I needed an army to leave.*

"Yeah."

"Are you still in love with me?"

"Sometimes."

"Sometimes," I said looking at him funny.

"Yeah, sometimes. You make it difficult to love you."

77

"I make it difficult to love me? But what about all the shit you do to me? Can you just answer one question for me?" I said sitting up in the bed facing him.

"What?' he said, all nonchalant.

"Why is it okay for you to do whatever you want to me, but I can't do one thing to you? You beat my ass, spit in my face, and held me hostage, but that doesn't mean shit to you because I forgot you can do whatever you want. Yes, I cheated with your brother and I'm sorry, but you have to forgive me for that especially since I have forgiven you for all the shit you've done to me."

"I don't have to do shit," he said turning his nose up at me. "And you know what? I'm done talking about this," he said, getting up and going in the bathroom. I got up and walked on the balcony. I needed some air. I loved and hated that nigga in the same breathe. I was glad I was leaving tonight. I looked through the door at the clock and it said 7:30. I smiled because it was almost time and in about 2 more hours I'll be out of this hell hole.

Chapter 6
Shynika

I sat on the couch and waited for my mom to come back out so she could explain what's been going on this past year. I was hurt by the fact that she didn't come see me in the hospital and I couldn't wait to hear this explanation. She finally came out of her room and sat next to me on the couch. "Hey baby," she said facing me.

"Hey."

"So where should I start?" she said taking a deep breathe.

"Let's start with you not coming to see me in the hospital. This whole time I've been thinking you didn't know and to find out that you did and just didn't come is fucked up," I said shaking my head.

"I wanted to come and see you, but I couldn't. I saw Tia at the store one day and she told me you were in the hospital. She said you had been in a coma, but you were alright. She said she would take me there, but I had to clean myself up first, but then I went and got high and the next thing I knew I had dozed off. I really did mean to come and see you, but the drugs just took over, but after that happened I knew it was time for me to get help.''

"Wait! So you saw Tia and she told you I was in the hospital?"

"Yeah."

"And you still didn't come? Even after she said I was in a coma?"

"Baby, you have to understand, I was in a fucked up place at that time in my life and I didn't know how to deal with it."

"So you let your only child lay up in the hospital, fighting for her life and you did not even come and show your face?" I yelled standing up.

"I'm sorry, but I didn't know how to be there for you at that time, but after that happened I went and checked myself into rehab. I went to a year treatment in Ohio so I could be there for you from that point forward. I've been getting myself together for you so I can be here for you now."

"So, why haven't I seen or heard from you since you've been back? After all, this was all done for me, right?" I said, waving my hands and turning up my lips.

"I just got discharged about a month ago and I wanted to make sure I was good and could live on my own clean before I came and seen you. I didn't want to get your hopes up to let you down again. I'm tired of disappointing you and I want to do everything I can to make it right. I love you."

"I love you, too," I said, giving my mom a hug. I learned a long time ago to not hold a grudge against her because she has a problem. I know my mom means well, but sometimes the drugs just take over her and at least she's trying and I'll give her that. I can't change the past but we can determine the future and I planned on being here for my momma and helping her kick this habit once and for all. "It's alright. I forgive you. I just hope it's for real this time," I said sitting back down.

"It is, I promise," she said, hugging me. "I love you more than any drug and I'm going to do the best I can to make it up to you. I know I can't get all those years back, but I plan on spending a lifetime trying," she said, letting me go.

"You don't need to spend time making up to me. All I want you to do is be there for me from this point forward. I'm going to give you a clean slate right now and if you fuck it up this time, I'm done."

"I won't."

"Good, now tell me about rehab," I said turning my body to face her.

"I don't know what you wanna know, but it was hell. I had the worst time of my life and I didn't know if I was going to make it or not, but every time I thought about quitting I would picture you and that would get me through the day. The worst part about it would have had to be the cold sweats and cravings."

"Do you still have cravings?" I asked.

"Every day and I don't think it will ever go away. Every day is a battle that I'm fighting within myself, but I refuse to lose."

"I'm proud of you, Mommy, and I'll be here for you in anyway."

"That's great, baby, but all I need you to do is keep doing what you're doing. I'm proud of you and all I need from you is a few more visits."

"I can do that. I can start coming down every other weekend."

"I'll love that," she said with a smile.

"Well, its set. I'll come down every other weekend." I stood up, hugged my mom, and walked in the kitchen. I grabbed something to drink. "I gotta go. I need to go check on Tia," I said walking back to the living room.

"What's wrong with her?"

"Nothing, she's just having relationship problems and she needs a friend."

"Yeah, you should do that. She was there for you and it's only right that you return the gesture."

I checked the clock and it was 4 o'clock. *She should be awake by now*, I thought as I walked back to my room to get my shoes. I grabbed my purse off the counter and headed out the door "I'll see you later" I said and closed the door behind me. I got in my car and drove around the corner to Tia's house. Her mom's car was in the driveway along with the car that was there earlier. I knocked on the door and her mom answered. "Hey Ms. Green, is Tia here?"

"Tia?" She looked at me with a puzzled look on her face. "You know Tia is in Chicago."

"She was in Chicago, but she called me last night and told me she was at your house," I explained to her.

"Well, I don't know when she was here because I haven't seen Tia in a few months. Is she driving that car right there?" she asked pointing at it.

"I don't know," I said, pulling out my phone and dialing Tia's number.

"Do you wanna come in?" she asked me.

"No, I'm fine. I'm just going to go home," I said as Tia's phone went to voicemail again. I left her another message and then went home to see if I could figure out how to find her. When I pulled up to my house my phone started ringing and it was a private number. "Hello."

"Hey girl, it's me," I heard somebody whisper and I knew it was Tia. We talked for a few minutes and she told me about how Ace came and got her and she was in Chicago. She also told me about her plan and how I had to get her brother and a few more people to help. I dialed Marcus's number.

"Hello?"

"What are you doing? I need your help," I said as soon as he said hello.

"You need my help doing what?" he said a little shocked.

"Tia is in trouble. She wants to come home but Ace won't let her so she needs us to go and get her."

"What you mean, he won't let her?"

"Just like I said. He's holding her hostage and we need to go get her."

"Do you know how to get there? I've only been there once and I don't remember."

"Yeah, I have the address. She said we should bring a few more people because Ace can be dangerous."

"I'm not scared of him or how dangerous he thinks he is but I'm not in town right now. I'm jumping on the highway now and I'll be there in an hour and a half. I'm coming straight to you, so be ready to go," he said before he hung up.

I sat in the car thinking about what Tia said about not getting the police involved and I was having second thoughts. *The man had killed somebody for God's sake and who's to say he won't do it again? I'm going to call the police and I don't care what Tia says, but I'll do it after she's safe*, I thought as I got out the car and went in the house to wait on Marcus to call me.

Marcus

I couldn't believe what Neek had just said. My sister was being held hostage in Chicago. I was confused because the guy that was holding her hostage was supposed to be her boyfriend. So, did they break up and he didn't want to accept the facts? I don't know, but whatever the reason was he wasn't about to be holding my sister against her will, doing whatever the fuck he wanted to her, and Neek had the nerve to say we were going to need more people because Ace was dangerous, like I was going to be scared of that little punk. Hell I could be just as dangerous as him if he pushed me. I sped down the highway, trying to get back to Kalamazoo as fast as I could. I was in Three Rivers handling business and I had to cut my meeting short. I got to Neek's house in about an hour and knocked on the door. Her mom answered and I must say she looked good. "Hey Ciera, how you doing?" *The last time I seen her she was strung out and looking like shit. I'm glad to see she's trying to clean herself up.* "Is Neek here?" I asked after staring at her for a few minutes.

"Hey, Marcus. I'm fine, how've you been?" she asked before letting me in. "Neek's in the back, Let me go and get her," she said closing the door and walking down the hall to her room. She opened the door and I could hear her tell Neek I was here and the next thing I knew Neek was walking in the living room.

"You ready?" she asked.
"Yeah."

"Alright, just let me grab my purse and then I'm ready. She walked back to her room and then returned. "I'm ready," she said walking toward the door. I got up, followed her out, jumped in the driver's side and we headed to Chicago.

Ace

I walked out the room because I was tired of putting up the Tia's mouth. "Who the fuck do she think she was talking to? Telling me that I have to forgive her sooner or later. I don't have to do shit," I repeated as I walked down the stairs to the kitchen. I was hungry so I decided to make me something to eat. *I guess I'll be nice and make Tia some since she just gave me some awesome head,* I thought, smiling just thinking about the way she just made me feel. I looked in the fridge and decided to make us a fried chicken for the salad while I cut up the lettuce and vegetables. I put both the salads together and headed up the stairs. When I reached the room Tia wasn't in there. I knew she was probably on the balcony since that was her favorite spot in the house. I walked out there and she was sitting in the lawn chair with a blanket.

I walked through the door. "Are you hungry?" I asked.

"I could eat. Why?"

"I made dinner. You can come in and eat when you're ready, but I suggest you come soon," I said and walked back in the room. I sat down on the bed and started eating my salad. Tia wasn't that far behind. She walked in the room and walked over to me. "Where's mine?" she said, looking at my food.

"Over there," I said pointing to the nightstand. She grabbed her food and came back to the bed and sat down.

"Thanks for the food," she said as she stuffed a huge bite in her mouth. "This is really good," she said taking another bite.

Tia

Ace is being nice, making me dinner and all, but there is no turning back at this point, I thought as I looked at the clock. It was 7:30 and I'd be leaving in no time. I finished eating my food and looked over at Ace, who was lying on the bed rolling a blunt. "Can I have my phone?" I asked, holding my hand out.

"What you need your phone for?" he asked never stopping what he was doing.

"Because it's my phone and I want it."

"You can get it when I feel you can behave."

"What the fuck you mean, when you feel I can behave? I'm not a damn child, Ace, and I want my phone!"

"Well, I'm not giving it to you. So, what are you going to do?"

"Nothing" I said and sat down on the bed. I was mad as hell but I couldn't woop him, trust me I already tried that. "Well, can I use your phone?" I said with an attitude.

"Why?"

"So I can let someone know that I'm alright. My mom is probably going crazy."

"Let them go crazy. You didn't give a fuck about letting me know you were alright."

"Come on, Ace. that's my mom."

He looked at me as if he was thinking about whether he wanted me to use his phone or not, and then finally reached in his pocket and gave it to me. "You have five minutes and you better not do something stupid."

I was about to get off the bed when Ace pulled me back down. "Where are you going?"

"To the bathroom."

"You don't have to go to the bathroom to talk on the phone."

"I know, but I had to pee" I said, trying to play it off. I really wanted to call Neek to see how far away she was.

"Well, go pee, but leave the phone here. You can make your call when you come back."

I put the phone on the bed and went to the bathroom. I really did have to pee so I wasn't lying about that. Ever since I became pregnant I swear I couldn't hold my pee for anything. I was sitting on the toilet try to think of another plan to get in contact with Neek, but it was no use. We didn't have a house phone; he had both cell phones and was watching me like a hawk. I finished up in the bathroom and walked out the door. Ace was still on the same spot and I walked over there and grabbed the phone and dailed my mom's number. I had to call her so Ace wouldn't get suspicious and think I was up to no good.

"Hey, Mom," I said when I heard her say hello.

"Hey, Tia. How are you?"

"I'm fine."

"Whose number is this? And why did Neek come over looking for you today? I thought you were still in Chicago."

Dig right in, I thought. "I am, Momma but I told Neek I was going to come today so that's probably why she was looking for me."

"So I guess this isn't your car in the driveway?"

"What car?" I asked as if I had no idea what she was talking about. I couldn't let her know I put that car there because then she would know I was lying about being there.

"There's a car in the driveway and I don't know how it got here."

"Maybe it's Marcus's."

"Yeah, maybe."

"Can you do me a favor and call Neek and let her know I'm alright? I don't want her to worry."

"What's wrong with your phone?"

"I lost it, but I have to go, Momma. I'll call you later," I said looking at Ace who was motioning his hands for me to hurry up.

"I love you, baby."

"I love you, too," I said and hung up the phone. I gave Ace back his phone, looked at the time, and decided to sit on the patio for an hour until my help came. I lay on the chair we had out there and read a book until I heard someone banging on the door. I got up, walked to the room, looked at the clock, and it was 9:30. I looked over at Ace who was sleeping then I heard the banging again. I ran out the room and down the stairs "I'm coming" I yelled to the people on the other side. I already knew it had to be Neek and them so I opened the door without asking who it was. "Why are y'all banging on the door like the damn police?" I questioned when I flung it open.

"We knocked lightly before and we didn't hear anybody coming" Neek said.

"I was sitting on the balcony and I heard y'all. Now be quite before Ace wakes up," I said, looking around to see if he was coming.

'That's too late," I heard him say. I turned around and saw him walking slowly down the stairs. "What's going on down here?"

"We came to get Tia," Neek said, putting her hand on her hip.

"You came to get Tia." He chuckled. "And where exactly do you think you're taking her?" he asked, stepping off the last step.

"We taking her home." Marcus wasn't saying anything, he was just standing there with a frown on her face.

"Tia's not going anywhere. Are you, Tia?" Ace asked.

"Umm…actually I am." I turned around and looked at Ace. "This is the end of us. I'm tired of living in this unhealthy relationship."

"What about my baby?' he said walking closer to me. My brother stepped in between the two of us and looked at me.

"Go get in the car," he said, looking me in the eyes. "We're done here and there's no need in explaining yourself."

I turned around and took a step toward the door, and then I heard Ace yell, "Don't you walk out that door, Tia! I swear I will find you…"

"And do what?" my brother yelled in his face. "You're not going to do shit to my sister and if you come near her again you're going to be sorry."

"Is that supposed to be a threat?" he asked walking up in my brother's face. I ran over and got in the middle of the two and looked at my brother. "Come on, let's just go," I said, trying to defuse the situation. The last thing I wanted was for my brother and Ace to start fighting. My brother looked at me for a minute, and then grabbed my arm and pulled me out the house. I locked eyes with Ace as Neek closed the door to what used to be my life, and I felt tears flowing down my cheeks. I wasn't sure how I was going to feel but this hurt more than I would have ever imagined. I felt like my heart was just torn in two. I got in the backseat of the car and cried silently.

Ace

I couldn't believe this shit. I wanted to punch Tia's brother right in his fucking face. *Who does he think he is? Coming in my house thinking he's running shit, but I'm going to play it cool today. Sometimes you have to lose a battle in order to win the war and I'll let them have this battle. I have to be smarter than what I'm thinking and not act on my emotions unless I wanted to catch a case, but believe me this shit is not over*, I thought as I headed back upstairs.

Neek

We left Ace's house and hit the highway. The car was silence except for Tia crying in the backseat. I felt bad for my friend; she was in love with this crazy ass nigga. *I could tell she really didn't want to leave which means she will probably be back, but not if I can help it*, I thought as I turned up the music and thought of a plan to get rid of Ace. We pulled up to a gas station so we could refuel. I got out of the car and went to the bathroom. I was going to wake Tia up, but she had just cried herself to sleep and we had

92

already stopped a few times for her to pee. I got in the bathroom and called the police, *this was my chance to make my call and maybe send Ace to prison and away from Tia*, I thought as I dialed 911.

"911, what's your emergency?"

"I would like to report a murder," I said through the receiver. I didn't know how I was going to prove Ace killed Mike, but at least I could start an investigation.

"Yes, can I have the location you're calling from?"

"109 Maple Street," I gave Ace's address.

"Is this where the murder took place?' the operator asked.

"No, but the person who committed the murder is at this address. His name is Anthony Ealy. I'm sorry, but that's all I know."

"Can I have your name, ma'am?"

"Shynika. I'm sorry, but I have to go," I said and hung up the phone. I walked out the bathroom. I didn't wanna be gone too long. When I got to the car Marcus was already in the driver's seat. "Dang, you took a long time."

"I wasn't gone that long, so stop it," I said through giggles.

"I filled up the tank and still had to wait on you."

"Oooh, well," I said as we drove back toward the freeway. I went on Facebook, looked up Tameka and sent her a message *Please call me when you can, it's important. 269 321 1234.*

Tameka

"Can I help you?" she asked when she opened the door and she didn't look all that sick to me.

"Hi, my name is Tameka and I'm Mike's girlfriend and he said he was here," I said, looking past her through the door.

"He said he was here?" she repeated with a puzzled look on her face. "Are you sure?"

"Yeah," I said shaking my head up and down.

"I'm sorry, why don't you come in and let's see if we can't straighten this out," she said stepping aside so I could walk in the house. I walked in and it was beautiful in there. She had a white furniture set with a brown coffee table. It was simple but classy. I sat on one of the sofas and I could see into the kitchen. There were brown lights hanging from the ceiling over the island in the center. The counters were brown to match the lights and it smelled like she was making popcorn earlier.

"Would you like anything to drink?" she asked still standing by the door.

"I'm okay."

"I'm sorry, but did I hear you correctly earlier? You're looking for my son," she said sitting down across from me.

"Yes, I haven't talked to him in a few weeks."

"And why do you think he's here?'

94

"Because the last time I heard from him he told me he was coming to visit you because you were sick."

"There must be some kind of mistake because I've been fine."

I can see that. "So you haven't seen Mike in the last month?" I asked

"No"

"Have you talked to him on the phone?"

"No, I haven't. I've called him a few times, but it keeps going straight to voicemail. I got a text from him, too, saying he needed to go out of town and he would call me when he could because he wasn't going to be able to be on his phone that much."

"Did he say where he was going or why?" I asked, trying to find some answers.

"No, it was through a text. I asked him a few question and I haven't heard from him since."

"I think something is wrong. This isn't like Mike to go this long without calling me and now that I know he's not here something really isn't right." I picked up my phone. "I'm calling the police," I said and dialed 911.

Ace

I was playing the game in the living room because I couldn't sleep when I heard someone pounding on the door. I thought it was Tia changing her mind because she knew she made a mistake. I opened the door and was met with a surprise. "Are you Anthony Ealy?" the tall, slim, and white officer asked.

"Yes, I am"

"I have some questions for you. Can I come in, please?"

"Do you have a warrant?" I hated the police and there was no way they were getting in this house without a warrant.

"No. Do I need one?"

"It depends. What is this all about?" I asked curious. *I know Tia didn't call the police on me*, I thought, but I hadn't hit her lately.

"This is about a murder," he said still standing in the doorway. "Now may I come in?" he asked again while his partner was just standing there with a smirk on his face.

"A murder!" *What the fuck was he talking about? I know he's not talking about Mike*, I thought. *But who could have told....that bitch Tia.* I stood there thinking about what he just said and wondering how much he knew. He couldn't know much because I know he don't have any evidence because I burned it all. "Who got murdered?" I asked.

"We're not sure yet. That's why I would like to ask you a few questions. Maybe you can come down to the station…"

"Wait…am I suspect?" I asked cutting him off.

96

"Mr. Ealy, I don't know anything until we ask you a few questions and get some more information."

"Well, come back here when you get some more information," I said and closed the door in thier face. Could Tia have really called the police on me and told them I killed Mike? I was pissed because I never seen this coming. I knew she hated me, but I never thought she would go to the cops and try to get me arrested. I sat back on the couch, rolled up and started thinking of a plan to eliminate this problem. *I have to get Tia back so I can make sure I have this under control, and after she had that baby I was going to shut that bitch up for good,* I thought as I hit my blunt and lent back.

Chapter 7
Tia

I lay in the backseat, crying the whole way home. We had to stop a few times because I had to use the restroom. We finally made it home around 2 in the morning and all I wanted to do was go to sleep. *I can't believe the day I just had*, I thought as I walked in my house and took my shoes off at the door. Marcus and Neek were right behind me.

"How long has this bullshit been going on?" Marcus asked me as he was walking in the house. This was the first time Marcus said something about my situation with Ace.

"Has what been going on?' I asked all confused.

"Don't play stupid with me. How long has that nigga been putting his hands on you?"

"Who said he was putting his hands on me?" *I've never told Marcus Ace was hitting me, so what makes him think that.*

"Tia, do you really think I'm stupid? I've been around a long time and I can sense when some shit's not right."

I looked down at the ground because I was ashamed. I didn't want my brother to ever find out about the abuse. "I don't feel like talking about it," I said, walking toward my room.

"Alright, but don't think we're not going to talk about this!" he yelled behind me. I didn't turn around. I walked in my room and lay across my bed with all my clothes on. A few minutes later I heard someone knocking at my door.

"Go away!" I yelled through the door. "I don't feel like being bothered."

"I'm not going anywhere," I heard Neek say, and then I heard the door open. I turned my head toward the door and saw her walking toward me. "Are you okay?" she asked as she sat on the bed next to me.

"Yeah, I'm fine."

"You know I'm always here for you if you need me," she said, rubbing my back.

"I know." I said, forcing a smile on my face. "But right now I would like to be by myself. I just need to sort some things out in my head."

"I understand," she said, standing up. "But I'm not leaving. I'll be in the living room sleeping on the couch if you need anything."

"Alright. Is Marcus still here?"

"No, he left," she said and walked toward the door.

"Where did he go?" I asked.

"He didn't say. He just said he would be back."

"Okay," I said and turned my head back toward the headboard.

"I love you," she said and walked out.

"I love you, too."

Tameka

We called the police and filed a missing person's report on Mike. They arrived at Dawn's house a few minutes after we called.

"When was the last time anyone has seen or talked to Mike?" the short black officer asked.

"We both received a text from him a few weeks ago, but no one has spoken to him," I answered.

"And what did the text say?" the officer asked while writing notes on his pad.

"Mine said he was coming to see his mom because she was sick, and hers said he was going out of town and would call when he can."

"Do you still have the messages?"

"I have mine," I said strolling through my phone trying to find it. I looked over at Dawn. "Do you still have yours?"

She was in a daze and couldn't believe that something could have happened to Mike. "I think so," she said slowly getting up and walking up the stairs. She came back down with her phone in her hand. "Yeah, I have it right here," she said and gave her phone to the officer. She sat back on the couch and didn't say another word.

"When's the last time anyone's seen him?'

"I saw him about a month ago at home. We live in Chicago and I left for a few days to visit my family and I haven't seen him since."

"You're from Chicago?"

"Yes."

"Okay, we'll contact the police there and see if we can't find out some information. I'm also going to take your phones to see if I can't find something out."

"How long would you need our phone?"

"I'm not sure, but here a number you can call for more information." The officer took our phones and asked us a few more questions and took a few more notes, and then asked for the most recent picture of Mike before he left.

"Thank you," I said and closed the door behind him. I turned around to look at Dawn who was still sitting on the couch in shock. "Are you okay?" I asked walking over to her.

"No, my son is missing," she said and started crying.

"I know, but we're going to find him." I sat next to her. "I'm sure he's alright," I said, trying to convince her as well as myself.

"I hope so. Mike and Ace are the only children I have and I would hate for something to happen to either one of them. Speaking of Ace, has anyone talked to him to see if he's heard from Mike?"

"I asked him and he said no. He did just get back from football camp also."

"I'm going to call him tomorrow and let him know what's going on."

"Yeah, you do that. I'm going to go to the room and get some rest. It's almost 2 in the morning," I said, looking at my watch. "I'll come over and check on you tomorrow before I head back home. I promise you I'm going to find out what happened to Mike and somebody is going to pay."

I gave her a hug and headed out the door. I couldn't believe Mike wasn't here. I was mad at him for not calling me and to think this whole time he's been missing. I felt horrible for not looking for him earlier. *What if somebody harmed him*, I thought, but not wanting to believe it. The thought of something happening to Mike brought tears to my eyes and I had to leave his mom's house before I started to break down. I left the house, got in my car, and cried.

I got to the hotel and checked my Facebook to see what was going on. I had a message from Neek, Tia's friend asking me to call her because it was important. It said she was active so I picked up the phone and dailed her number.

"Hello" she answered.

"Hey, is this Neek?"

"Who is this?' she asked with an attitude.

"This Tameka."

"Oh, hey Tameka. You got my message?"

"Yeah, what do you have to tell me that's so important?"

"Mike killed Ace" she said getting straight to it.

"What do you mean Mike killed Ace?" I asked confused.

"You heard me. Mike killed Ace and I just called the police and told them. Tia is going to be mad because she didn't want me to so that's why I contacted you.'

"And you know this for a fact?"

"Yes, but I can't prove it."

"And how did he do it?" I asked still a little skeptical.

"I'm not sure but he did and I bet you won't ever see Mike again. Think about it, when's the last time you seen Mike?"

I thought about it for a minute and it wasn't adding up. Ace and Mike were bestfriends, hell more like brothers so why would he kill him? "I'm going to sleep on it and we can discuss this more tomorrow." I hung up the phone, got in the shower and went to sleep thinking about Mike and what could have happened to him.

Tia

I woke up the next morning and walked out my room. Neek was sleeping on the couch. I started to wake her up, but I decided against it. I went in th kitchen and started making breakfast. I made some pancakes, bacon and eggs and woke her up for breakfast. "Neek" I said shaking her shoulder. I saw her eyes open and close before she sat up.

"What's up, Tia, is something wrong?" she asked, looking around.

"No, nothing is wrong. I just made us breakfast."

"You woke me up for breakfast?" she asked, looking irritated. "What time is it?"

"It's almost 10."

"It's only 10. I need a few more hours," she said, laying back down. "Wake me up at 1. I'm going back to sleep." She pulled the cover over her face and closed her eyes.

"I guess I'll just put your food in the microwave."

"Yeah, do that!" she yelled from under the covers. "And don't wake me up anymore unless it's an emergency."

I walked into my mom's room and nobody was there. I wondered where my mom was. It was Tuesday so she was probably at work. I ate my food and went back in my room to read a book. *I need to escape this madness called my life and there is no better way than to read a good book*, I thought as I read *Bitch* and lost myself in *Precious*. I was interrupted a few hours later by Neek walking through the door. She walked over and sat next to me in my bed.

"Are you okay?" she asked.

"I'm fine," I said, putting my book down.

"You know you don't have to front for me."

"I know and I'm not. I mean I'm not going to lie I'm heartbroken, but I know this is the best thing for me and my baby," I said, rubbing my stomach. "Ace wasn't right and I didn't need to raise my baby in that unhealthy environment."

"Isn't that the truth and don't worry about your baby because it's going to be well taken care of" she said rubbing my stomach. "TT Neek is going to take care of her baby, yes she is" she said talking to my stomach.

"I know but I just feel bad about the fact that Ace isn't going to be involved."

"He doesn't deserve to be involved, fuck him. We can do this by ourselves."

"No it's not a fuck him. He's the father of my child and despite what I think about him he still deserves the right to be here."

"If you say so, but I think you should leave him where he's at."

"Whatever!" I said irritated. "Did you want something or did you just come in here to talk about my baby's father?"

"Yes, I want something. I was thinking last night and I think you should come back to campus with me."

"Come back to campus with you? I don't go to school there, so what am I going to do?"

"You can stay with me and enroll next semester."

"You live in a sorority house. How am I going to stay with you?"

"You can stay there for a little while, and then we can get our own apartment."

"I don't know about that," I said, shaking my head.

"Well, you can't stay here."

"Why not?"

"Because Ace will find you here and he'll come and take you right back to Chicago. You need to go somewhere where he can't get you."

I thought about what she said for a minute and she was right. I needed to go somewhere where Ace couldn't find me if I wanted to live a free life because if he ever got me back to Chicago I was never going to be able to leave now, especially after this shit I just pulled last night. "When are you leaving?" I asked.

"Next week. I want to spend some time with my mom before I go back to campus."

"Your mom? How she's doing?' I asked.

"She's fine. She's been clean for almost a year now."

"She's clean?" I said in shock

"Yeah, she said she went to rehab and really wanted to get her life together this time."

"That's great, Neek. What made her do it?" I asked.

"Not being there for me when I needed her the most. Why didn't you tell me you seen my mom and told her I was in a coma?"

"I was going to surprise you, but when I went to pick her up she didn't show. I didn't want to tell you because you had already been through a lot."

"I understand, but you were the reason for her going to rehab. That day she didn't show up she was getting high. She felt really bad about not being there for me and went to rehab the next day."

"That's good because I looked all over for her that day and when I found her she promised she would be ready later and I waited for an hour and she never showed. I couldn't understand why she didn't show, but drugs will make you do some crazy things. I'm glad she's better and I hope she stays clean for the long haul."

"Me too."

Ace

Almost two weeks had gone by since Tia had left and called the police on me. I still couldn't believe they showed up at my house, asking me about a murder. *Could she really had told them that I killed Mike?* I wondered. I just don't believe she would have done that, but who else could have done it but her? She was the only witness. I had gone to her mom's house a few times looking for her, but she was never there. I didn't want to knock on the door because I'm pretty sure she told her mom about what happened. I guess she got smarter and realized that hiding out at home was not a good idea. I also went by Neek's house and I didn't see anything. I decided it would be better to go back home since Football season was about to start next week.

I jumped on the highway and headed home, the whole time thinking about where Tia could be. I needed to find her and my baby before this thing gets out of hand. She's upset with me right now and she might do something she can't take back. I had no way of getting in contact with her since she blocked me from all Social Medias and calling her along with Neek. I guess I would have to hire a P.I. to find her and this time I had to find something permanent to do with her. I couldn't kill her yet, but believe me when she has that baby her ass is dead. I pulled up to my house and I couldn't believe my eyes. There were police cars everywhere and they were searching my house. "What the fuck is going on?" I screamed as I got out the car.

"Are you Anthony Ealy?" one of the officers asked.

"Yes, I am."

"We have a warrant for your arrest," he said, handing me the warrant.

Tia

I was scrolling through the channels when I came across the news that read, NFL player arrested for murder. The headline got my attention and I couldn't help but watch, but what I wasn't prepared for was the player was that was being charged with the crime. They didn't have any more details and said he'd be getting arraigned tomorrow morning. I put down the remote and Googled Ace to see if I could find out any more information and I got nothing. *I have to go and see what was going on*, I thought as I grabbed my phone and dialed his number private. He didn't answer but it didn't go straight to voicemail, which let me know he wasn't in jail; if he was in jail then his phone would have gone straight to voicemail. I called again and still no answer. I must have called five times and still nothing. Ace doesn't answer private calls because he says "If I can't see who's calling then you don't need to talk to me". I tried his number one more time, but this time I called straight through and he answered on the second ring. "Hello!"

"Hello, is the Ace?"

"Who is this?"

I really didn't want to tell him who I was, but I know he probably wasn't in the mood to play games. "It's me."

"Tia?"

"Yeah."

"You have some nerve calling my fucking phone," he said cold through the phone.

"Why you say that?"

"Don't try to act like you don't know what's going on."

"What are you talking about?" I asked stunned. "I didn't do anything."

"So, you didn't call the police?"

"No, I didn't call the police. Why would I do that? I was calling to check on you and see what's going on."

"Well somebody did something, but it's not something I can talk about over the phone."

"Can I come and see you?'

"Why?"

"I wanna make sure you're alright. I love you and I would never do anything to harm you, but if you don't want me to come I won't."

"You can come if you want. We need to talk anyways."

"Alright, I'm on my way. I'm leaving now."

I grabbed my suitcase and started packing a few clothes. I caught a glimpse of myself in the mirror. I was starting to show, but I didn't look like I was four months. I stood there, thinking about the fact that I never got the chance to enjoy my pregnancy. I'd spent the whole time dealing with this Ace's bull. I shook that out of my head and kept packing. I grabbed a note and let Neek know I had to go and check on Ace. I knew she wouldn't agree, but this was the father of my child and I had to make sure he was alright.

I jumped in the car and headed to Chicago. I wondered who the hell was able to tell on Ace. *I know I didn't call the police and nobody knew about what happened to Mike but the two of us*, and then I thought about it. *I told Neek, but she wouldn't have called the police on Ace, would she?* I thought as I was driving down I-94. *She didn't like Ace and she would do anything to get him out of my life, so maybe she did call the police on Ace, but why wouldn't she tell me? My mind was racing a thousand miles per minute and I didn't know what to do. They couldn't have a case because she didn't know enough to tell them details and it's not like I'm going to testify. Oh man, Ace thinks it's me that told on him but I can't tell him I told Neek. He's going to want to make sure she could never tell and we all know what that means.*

It took me another hour before I got to Ace's house and I was trying to think of what I was going to say the whole time. I couldn't tell on my best friend, but I knew when I got here it was not going to be pretty. *He wouldn't hurt me, would he? Naw he already told me that as long as I'm pregnant I'm good*, I thought I as pulled up to the gate. My stomach was flipping and it was not because of the baby. I was scared and I couldn't stop my hands from shaking as I was putting in the code. I pulled up in front of the house and took a deep breath.

Shynika

I leaned my head back and enjoyed the pleasure Nate was giving me. He was sucking on my clit and sticking his finger in and out of my hole at the same time. "Damn, that feels good," I whispered as I took his head and pushed it further in my spot. He removed his hands, spreading my lips apart and put his tongue in the same spot his fingers were at. He took his tongue in and out of my hole, first moving slowly and then speeding up the pace. I started rotating my hips in a circle and pushing my clit in his face. He was taking my body to pure ecstasy. I felt my back starting to arch as I pushed my hips off the bed. He started sucking on my clit and it started going crazy. "Oh my gosh, I'm coming…" I screamed as I felt my body heating up. I felt the cum draining out of my body as I passed out.

"Damn you taste good," he said, climbing on top of me.

"I'm glad I didn't disappoint you."

"I knew you wouldn't," he said, touching me clit. "Let my little man get some of this," he said rubbing my clit with his pipe.

I took his pipe and was about to put it in, but I heard something on the TV that caught my attention. "NFL player charged with murder."

"What did he say?" I asked pushing him off me.

"What did who say?" he said confused.

"The TV, what did the TV say?"

"I don't know and I don't care," he said, kissing me on the neck.

"Well I do. Now, it said something about a NFL player being arrested for murder."

"Oh yeah, that nigga, Ace. He use to go here and now he plays for Chicago. He got arrested yesterday for murder, but he's out now. Why you concerned about that anyway? What you know the nigga or something?"

"Actually I do." I said getting up. "I have to go." I grabbed my clothes, put them on and headed for the door.

"So, you're just going to leave us like this?" he yelled.

"I'll call you...I'm sorry!" I yelled back as I walked out the door. I jumped in my car and dialed Tia's number. She didn't answered. I started up the car and dialed her number again. I still didn't get an answer. I locked at the time and it was 3 in the

113

morning. She was probably sleeping. I pulled away from the curb and headed home. It took me an half an hour and when I got there I didn't see Tia's car. We moved out of the sorority house and got a three bedroom for us and the baby. We had only been living there for a week, but Tia's usually didn't go anywhere. I entered the house, went in her room and it was empty. I was about to leave and turn off the light when I noticed a note on her nightstand. I walked over, picked it up and noticed it was addressed to me. I opened it and couldn't believe what I had just read. Tia said she was going to Chicago to check on Ace because he was being charged with murder. I picked up my phone and dialed her number again and there was still no answer. I called a few more times before I went in my room to lay down. *There is nothing I can do about it today,* I thought as I closed my eyes and I was dead to the world.

I woke up the next morning and called Tia, and she still didn't answer. I couldn't believe she went back to see that nigga after everything we did to get her here. I was pissed and I was getting tired of him. It's like he had some kind of hold on her that she couldn't seem to shake. I had to find a way to get rid of him for good. *I'm going to call Katrice and see if we can't put our original plan into action. Ace has to go and I don't care what I have to do to do it.* I picked up the phone and dialed Katrice's number.

"Hello."

"Hey, girl, what you doing?"

"Nothing, about to jump in the shower."

"Can we meet up later? I wanna talk to you about something."

"What?"

"I would rather do it in person."

"Alright, we can meet up in an hour. I'll text you details."

"Alright," I said and hung up. I talked to Katrice sometimes, but not much since Tia's been here, but now we both had a common hate and we both had a piece to each other's puzzle.

Katrice

Neek and her friend Tia had been on campus for over 2 weeks and what I couldn't believe was that the bitch was pregnant. She had gone and gotten knocked up by my man and I was pissed. Ace was always careful and made sure he used a condom so there was no way any girl could get pregnant unless he wanted her too. I had tried for a year to have Ace's baby and he wasn't going. I couldn't stand the sight of her and every time I saw her I wanted to knock that baby out of her.

Neek wanted to meet me today so we could catch up and she had to ask me something. I really didn't want to meet up with her, but I wanted to see what she had to say. I still wanted to find out where Ace was and see if I could get him back, since he and

Tia were on bad terms which meant he was back on the market. I got in the shower and prepared to meet Neek. I texted her the address to this restaurant downtown. I heard good things about it and I was hungry, so I would be killing two birds with one stone. I was the first to arrive. I walked in and it was small and cozy. There was an open table along the wall by the window. I walked over and had a seat. When the waitress came over I ordered water for the both of us and waited on Neek. Five minutes later I saw her walking up through the window; she was walking fast like someone was chasing her.

"Hey girl," she said and slid in her seat.

"Hey."

"Did you hear the news?" she asked.

"What news?"

"Well I was watching the news early this morning and I saw that Ace got arrested."

"Ace got arrested? My Ace?" I asked with my hand on my chest.

"If that's what you want to call him, but yeah, that Ace."

"And what the fuck is that supposed to mean?"

"Nothing," she said rolling her eyes.

I know this bitch was not trying to be cool, or I would slap the fuck out of her. "What he get arrested for?" I asked dropping the comment she just made.

116

The waitress came over and took our order. Neek
didn't order anything, but I went in.

"They said murder," she said when the
waitress walked away.

"Murder," I said in shock. "Who the fuck did
he kill?"

"I don't know. I Googled it and I couldn't
find out any more information."

"So, you called me here to tell me that Ace is
locked up for murder?"

"No, I called you here to see if we can't
continue our plan. Tia went back to Chicago to be
with Ace because she said she had to be there for her
man, but he isn't right, especially now since he's
facing murder charges. I don't want her to get caught
back up with him and I want him out of the picture
permanently."

"Why? He's about to go to jail for murder."

"That's not a guarantee, plus if he goes to jail
I feel like Tia is going to want to be there for him
more since that *is* her baby daddy and all."

"So, what do you want me to do about it?" I
said a little out of it. I was still thinking about the fact
that Ace was in jail. "She went and seen him in jail?"

"I want you to get your cousin back on the
job...and no, he's home now. He bonded out."

"Do you have the address now?"

"Yeah, I got it."

"Give it to me" I said holding out my hand.

"Not until I know the plan and we both are on the same page."

"Alright, I will get in touch with my cousin and let you know." I said as the waitress brought over my food.

"Alright, the sooner the better," she said, stood up, and walking toward the door. I was going to get Ace's address, but not to kill him. *I still want him back and this is the perfect time to be there for him. I'll be taking this address and paying him a personal visit.*

Chapter 8
Ace

I heard a knock at the door and I knew it had to be Tia. I was debating on whether or not to open it, but I had just talked to her. I got off the couch and walked over to the door. I took a deep breath and opened it.

"Hey," she said, standing on the step.

"What's up?"

"Nothing, I came to check on you. Are you going to let me in?"

"Yeah," I said, moving to the side. She was starting to show and her face was getting fatter, but it looked good on her. She walked past me and her ass was getting bigger, too. I smiled and licked me lips. "You getting thicker" I said smiling.

'You mean fatter."

"Naw, I meant thicker. You're looking good."

"Thank you," she said, sitting on the couch.

I closed the door, walked over to the couch, and sat next to her. "I missed you," I whispered in her ear.

"What did you miss about me, Ace? Treating me like shit?" she said with and attitude.

"Naw, I'm missed the way you smell and how soft your skin is. I missed your smile and just being able to watch you walk around here."

"Sounded good."

"What the fuck you mean, sounded good?"

"Just like I said, sounded good. I'm not falling for this shit again. Now let's be real. Why are you being so nice to me tonight? What do you think I told on you?"

Just the thought that she told on me made me want to fuck her up, but I had to play it cool because I really did want some of the pussy. I leaned in and started kissing her on her neck. "I really did miss you," I said, creeping my hand under her shirt. I undid her bra and released her firm 34 Bs. "You didn't miss me?" I asked, pulling her to my chest. I grabbed one of her breasts in each hand and started squeezing them. I sucked on her neck then pulled her shirt over her head. I took off the rest of her clothes and spreaded her legs open. I got on my knees and lined my lips up with her lips and went to work. I took my time sucking on her ring and putting my tongue in and out of her hole. I sucked on her clit like it was a sucker and then stuck two fingers in her hole and fingered and sucked her until she came. I got up and took my clothes off. She was laying back on the

120

couch with a smile on her face. "What you smiling for?"

"That shit felt good" she said still smiling from ear to ear.

'Let me make you feel even better," I said, climbing on top of her. I slid my pipe in her hole and it was wet and tight just like I like it. When I slid it in she jumped a little and from the way it felt I knew she hadn't been giving my goods away. "Ohh, this feels good," I whispered in her ear as I was rotating my hips in a circle. I felt her grinding back and I started going in. I threw her legs over my shoulder and started pounding in her wet spot, the more I pounded the wetter she got "Damn, baby, this shit is extra wet...I guess it's true what they say: pregnant pussy is the best pussy," I said, going deeper and deeper.

"I love you Ace" she said digging her nails in my back.

"I love you too" I said kissing her in the mouth. The truth was I really did love Tia and despite all the bullshit she's done I couldn't stop thinking about her the whole time she was gone. I really wanted to give her a second chance and see about having a family sometimes. I started playing with her ring with my fingers, this shit drives her crazy and going deeper at the same time, and then I felt her back start to arch and I already knew what time it was. I gave her long strokes through her orgasm until she passed out.

"Turn over," I said, pulling out of her. She turned over and threw her arms over the couch. I slid in her and went as hard as I could on her until I released all my babies in her guts. "I love you," I said and kissed her on the back. I slid out and walked up stairs.

Tia

I couldn't believe Ace had just fucked the shit out of me like that and he kissed it. I was on the couch stuck and I mean literally. I lay there for a few more minute before I finally got up and went to the bathroom. I peed and headed upstairs. When I reached the room Ace was in the shower. I sat on the bed and looked at the closet. All my stuff was still there like I left it. I was surprised to see he hadn't touched anything. He must have thought I was coming back or something. I heard the shower go off then a few minutes later Ace came out wearing nothing but a towel and the man looked sexy as hell. He walked over the bed and sat on the edge. "Can I take a shower?" I asked.

"Why did you ask me?"

"I don't live here anymore, so I was being polite."

"You still have a key, don't you?"

"Yeah."

"Then you still live here. Stop acting brand new and get your ass in the shower."

I got up and walked in the bathroom. I turned on the shower and enjoyed the hot water hitting my skin. *I missed this shower*, I thought as I stood there enjoying the mini massage. I got out the shower, dried off, and went back in the room. Ace was still sitting on the bed with no clothes on. I walked over to him and cuddled up next to him in what used to be my spot. "So, what happened? Why did you get arrested?"

"They had a warrant for my arrest and they said it was for murder."

"Did they say if it was Mike or not?"

"No they didn't, Tia, but that's the only person it could be so I'm going to ask you: did you call the police on me?" he asked, raising my chin and looking me in the eye.

"No, Ace, I would never do that to you."

"Then how do they know? Did you tell someone?"

I knew I had told Neek, but I didn't want her to get involved in this so I lied. "No, I didn't tell anyone," I lied and dropped my eyes.

"You're lying, Tia. Now I'm going to ask you again. Did you tell anyone?"

"Nobod..." I tried to say before he was on top of me with his hand around my throat.

"Why must you lie all the time?"

"I'm not lying," I whispered but could barely get out.

"Yes, you are. now tell me who the fuck you told before I snap your fucking neck. The baby won't matter to me when I serving 25 to life," he said, squeezing my neck harder. I didn't want to get Neek involved, but I had to think about my unborn child.

"Neek," I whispered.

"What you say?" he asked, letting go of my neck.

"I told Neek," I said rubbing my neck.

"You told your noisy ass friend that already doesn't like me. What the fuck were you thinking?" he screamed in my face.

"I was thinking about the fact that you had just killed a man and that I might be next. I was trying to protect me and my unborn baby," I said rubbing my stomach.

"And you thought telling her was going to do what?"

"Well, if something happened to me she was supposed to go to the police."

"Do you think she went to the police anyways?"

"I don't know but I don't think she would, considering that she knows how much I love you and you are the father of my child....naw, I don't see her doing that," I said trying to convince him more than me.

"Well, my lawyer said somebody called in and reported a murder. They didn't say who I killed, but they gave my name and address."

"Are you serious?" I asked in shock.

"Dead. Somebody is definitely out to get me and I think it's your best friend. Now the question is what should I do about it?"

"Nothing, it's not like she knows anything. They don't have any evidence against you and I'm sure as hell not going to testify."

"I don't think so. I already got suspended off the team until further notice and it's all because of that bitch and you telling me I should just let it ride?"

"No, I'm telling you to be smart. Think about it. The police have to know she's the one that reported the crime. Now if she comes up missing, who's going to be the first person they suspect? You and then they really won't stop until they lock you up so like I said do nothing and after this is all over and you're cleared you can just let it go. They can't have that much evidence."

"You're right, but I'm telling you this right now I'm not letting shit go," he said and pulled his weed out the drawer and started breaking it down. "And you're right they don't have any evidence, that's why they couldn't hold me. I didn't get out on bond. I got out because they didn't find anything when they searched my house so they can't stick anything to me." He rolled his blunt, lit it, and leaned back against the headboard.

"I'll talk to her, too," I said and kissed him on the cheek.

Shynika

I left from seeing Katrice and I felt good about what I was planning. Ace was finally about to get what he deserves. I tried to call Tia again, but I still didn't get an answer. I went to the house to see if she was back, but she wasn't there either. I was worried about her and there was nothing I could do at this time except drive to Chicago and I wasn't doing that just yet. I rolled up and watched TV until I passed out. I woke up to my phone ringing and it was Tia. *At least I know she's alright now*, I thought as I answered. "Hello."

"Hey, girl. What you doing?"

"Nothing, where you at? I've been calling you all day."

"I'm in Chicago. Did you see the news? I know you know what happened to Ace."

"Yeah, I saw it."

"You sure all you did was seen it?"

"What do you mean by that?" I asked, turning my nose up.

"What I said. Are you sure all you did was seen it? Did you also set it all up?"

"Meaning?" I asked, playing dumb. I knew exactly what she was asking, but I didn't want to admit to anything.

"Did you call the police on Ace?"

I wanted to lie, but there was no need. it was going to come out that I did it so I might as well confess. "Yeah. I called."

"Why? Why would you want to send my baby's father to jail for murder?"

"I called because I want him as far away from you as possible. Ace is no good for you and you need to see that."

"Trust me I know Ace is not perfect. I know I need to leave him alone and I plan on it, but I don't need you butting in and I definitely don't want to see him in jail."

"Ohh, so now you don't need me butting in?" I asked confused. "Just a few weeks ago you needed me butting in."

"And that was a mistake. If I hadn't of had you in my business you wouldn't have been able to call the police and tell them anything."

"Well, excuse me for trying to help my friend," I said sarcastically. "That nigga must really got you brained washed but you don't have to worry because it will *never* happen again."

"Nobody got me nothing so you can stop with that. I was doing just fine by myself these last few weeks and you know it."

"But you also went running back the first chance you got."

"You are a liar, I came back because of something you did. He needs somebody here for him and I plan on being that person. After all he was the one that was by my side when you were in that coma or did you forget?"

"I didn't forget, but don't let him hold that over your head forever."

"He's not holding shit over my head but whatever you say. I'm done with this conversation....goodnight," she said and hung up the phone. I knew I pissed her off, but somebody needed to tell her and what kind of friend would I be if I didn't let her know when she's caught up? I hated Ace with a passion and that conversation, the way she was defending him just turned my stomach upside down. He definitely had to go.

Tia

I couldn't believe all that shit Neek was just talking on the phone. I hated when people were all in my business, but I know what she was saying was right. I needed to leave Ace alone and move on with my life, but that didn't give her the right to try to send him to jail for murder. I couldn't believe she would do that and to think I told her that in confidence that she wouldn't tell anybody else. Not only did she tell somebody else, but she told the fucking police, and

Keyanna Ford

this made me question our friendship and if I could trust her or not.

I got off the chair and walked back in the room. Ace was in the bed watching TV and I didn't know if I should tell him about our conversation or not. I sat next to him and got under the covers. I decided not to tell him anything because even though I felt Neek was wrong for doing that shit behind my back, I didn't want her being on his hit list. I loved that girl and I knew if the shoe was on the other foot I would be doing anything in my power to get her out of a fucked up relationship. I knew she only wanted the best for me and I couldn't fault her for that. I should have known better than to tell her about that situation and this was my fault. *I have to figure out a way to make this right*, I thought as I scooted closer to Ace. I also needed to find a way to fall out of love with this character.

"What did she say?" he asked and wrapped his arms around me.

"She said she didn't say anything to anyone," I lied.

"She's lying. She's the only person who could have told, or you're lying and you told."

"Well, I didn't lie and I didn't call the police on you. I swear," I said rolling over to face him.

"I believe you, but I don't believe Neek."

"I'm sorry I even told her," I said shaking my head. "But I was mad and it just came out."

"You shouldn't have never let no shit like that come out."

"I know. Can't we just drop it? After all you're not in jail."

"That's because they don't have enough evidence, but that doesn't mean they're going to stop looking and on top of everything I can't even play this fucking season. So no we can't just drop it."

"Well, I'm going to drop it because I didn't come here for this. I came here to make sure you were alright not to argue. I was having a good day, the sex was good, and I just want to enjoy this moment," I said as I rolled over.

"I'm glad to see somebody's enjoying themselves," he said sarcastically.

"Whatever," I said, waving my hand and closing my eyes.

Tameka

I woke up the next day hoping I was dreaming. I couldn't believe Mike wasn't at his mom's house. *Where could he be?* I thought as I walked in the bathroom and turned on the shower. Not to mention the phone call I had with Neek, I really didn't want to believe her but she could be telling the truth. I needed to get dressed so I could go and buy me another cell phone since mine's was classified as "evidence". I jumped in the shower, got dressed, and headed out the door. I Googled a Sprint store and was on my way. A few hours later I was holding a brand new phone in my hand with the same number. I also got Dawn a phone because they took hers, too. I headed over to her house to check on her, but when I arrived there was a police car outside of her house. Butterflies formed in my stomach because what could they have found out in a day? *Is this good news or bad news?* I thought as I knocked on the door and waited a few minutes.

"Who is it?" I heard Dawn say.

"Tameka."

She opened the door. "Hey, Tameka, I'm glad you're here," she said opening the door. "Come on in, I didn't know how to get a hold of you. The officer is here and he said he might have some information," she said moving to the side and waving me in.

I walked in. "They have some information already?" I asked in shock. "But it's only been a day."

"I know, but he said they had something reported in Chicago today and it might be linked to Mike, but I'll let the officer explain. He just got here and was about to explain it to me," she said walking over to the couch, sitting down next to him. *I'm glad to see she's better than she was yesterday*, I thought as I followed her to the couch.

"How you doing?" I asked the officer.

"I'm doing alright."

"That's good. Now, are you here to deliver good or bad news?" I asked, sitting down.

He let out a long sigh and I knew it couldn't be good. "I got in contact with the Chicago police and gave them all the information you gave me. Well, they called me back today and said they got a phone call from a woman saying a man killed someone and gave the killers information and address then hung up. They tracked the ladie down and got some more information and she didn't know much but she did eventually say the victim name was Mike. She said her bestfriend boyfriend did it but she didn't know why because they were best friends. *He was talking about Neek. I was going to tell him about our phone call last night but if it was Ace he was going to pay.*

"Mike, not my Mike?" I asked in shock. I looked at Dawn and I saw tears forming in her eyes.

"She didn't know Mike's last name, but she said her friend told her that her boyfriend killed him."

"What's the other's guy name?" I asked still not believing that my Mike could be gone.

"They guy being accused of the crime is Anthony Ealy."

"Anthony Ealy!" Dawn said in shock. "That can't be right, Ace and Mike are like brothers."

"You'll be surprised how many people are killed by the ones they love," the officer said, looking

132

Keyanna Ford

at Dawn. "But she did say they were best friends" he repeated.

"Do they really think Ace killed Mike?" Dawn asked in shock.

"I'm not sure, but for right now this is all we have to go on."

"I just don't believe this," she said, shaking her head over and over.

"I know it's hard to believe, but finding out the truth is better than not knowing. We're not sure if this is your Mike, but I just wanted to come over here and let you know what we've found out. I'll keep you guys posted and you'll be able to get your phones back as soon as possible," he said standing up. "Thank you for your time and I pray that we find Mike alive," he said, extending his hand.

"Thank you for stopping by and keeping us posted," I said shaking his hand. I walked him to the door, closed it and when I turned around Dawn was sitting on the couch in a daze.

"Are you alright?" I asked walking over and sitting next to her on the couch.

"No, I don't understand why Ace would kill Mike. They are practically brothers and this doesn't sound right."

"I have no idea," I stated honestly. "But I hope this is not our Mike they are talking about."

"I'm going to call Ace right now," she said, reaching for the phone.

133

"No, don't do that," I said, grabbing it from her. "We don't want him to know that they're on to him. What if he destroys some of the evidence?" I said, trying to make sure that if Ace was the one that he would get what was coming for him. She reluctantly put the phone back on its base and started crying. I felt bad for Dawn because I knew how she was feeling. I loved Mike, too, and I also wanted to cry, but I felt I had to be strong for her. I wrapped my arms around her, rubbed her back, and let her let it out.

"I know this is hard, but we don't even know if it's him yet," I said, trying to make her feel better.

"Something's not right and I can feel it," she said between tears. "It's been almost a month and nobody has talked to him. Something is definitely wrong." I wanted to say something, but I couldn't because I felt the same way; something was wrong. *This isn't like Mike to go this long without talking to someone,* I thought as I continued rubbing her back and listening to her cry. This shit broke my heart and I felt tears forming in my own eyes. I sat there listening to her cry for a few more minutes, and then she stood up. "I'm going to go to bed," she said, wiping her face.

"Are you going to be okay?"

"Yeah, I'll be fine."

"Are you sure?"

"Yeah."

"Alright, I got you this phone," I said, handing it to her. "And I already programmed my number in it. Feel free to call me whenever. I don't care what time of day it is, you can call me."

"Okay," she said and took the phone.

"I'm going home today, but if you need me I can stay longer."

"Thank you but I'll be fine."

"If you say so," I said, giving her a hug. "It'll be alright," I whispered in her ear.

"I hope so."

I walked toward the door, opened it, and gave her one last hug before I walked out. I couldn't believe the officer said they think Ace killed Mike, but why was my question. I wanted to call and confront Ace, but I had to take my own advice I had just gave Dawn. I started up my car and headed to the hotel to gather my few items before it was time for my flight.

It'd been two weeks since I came back from seeing Mike's mom and every day I wanted to go over to Ace's house and confront him, but I knew better. I had to be smart about this and if Ace did do it he was going to pay was all I kept thinking. I was at home, which was weird considering this was Mike's house, flipping through the channels when I came across some breaking news. The headline read: *NFL Player Arrested for Murder*. This caught my eye because I wanted to know if it was Ace or not and when they showed a picture of the player which was Ace I knew he was getting arrested for the murder of Mike. I picked up the phone and dialed Dawn's number. The phone rang a few times before she finally answered

"Hello," she said in a low raspy voice.

"Hi, how are you doing? I asked

"I'm alright."

"That's good. I was calling to check on you and to see if you watched the news lately?"

"No, I haven't watched the news. Actually I haven't been doing too much of anything lately."

"I can understand that," I said in agreement. "But I just so happened to be flicking through the channels today and I came across a report saying that Ace got arrested today for murder."

"Ace got arrested for murder?" she asked in shock.

"Yes, so this must mean that they've found some more information."

"I just can't believe this. Did it say if they found the body or not?" she asked through tears.

"No it doesn't say, but I can imagine that they would contact you if they did. It didn't say much but that Ace was arrested and they're searching his home for evidence."

"Yeah, you're right. So they really think he did it. This just seems so surreal to me."

"Me too. I've known Ace for the same amount of time that I've been with Mike and I would have never thought he would do something like this."

"Me either. Hell, I took him in when he was little and raised him as my own. They're more than friends; they're like brothers so I don't know what could have happened to cause this. I wanna talk to Ace so he could tell me why."

"I would love to know, too, but then again I don't because nothing he says is going to bring Mike back if in fact he is dead."

"You're right, Tameka, and I can see why my son loved you."

I smiled through the phone. "Thank you, I'm just sad we had to meet like this."

"Me too. I'm sorry, but I have another call that I have to take. I'll call you back later or call me if you get some more information."

"I'll do that," I said and hung up the phone.

Chapter 9
Katrice

I called Neek two days later and told her that my cousin was still down to do the job, but that I needed the address. She gave it to me this morning. I packed a bag, put on my face, and got ready to get my man back. I walked out the door and got in the car ready to get my man back. I was nervous because Ace and I didn't end on the best of terms. I took a few deep breaths and got myself together. I started the car and headed toward the highway. I went by myself and didn't let anyone know I was going. I didn't want to give them the opportunity to try and talk me out of it. I looked at the clock and it was 3pm. I checked the GPS when I hit I-94. It said it took about 4 hours to get to his address. I lit one of my pre-rolled blunts, put the car in cruise control, and enjoyed the ride.

It was a quarter past 7 and the GPS said I was less than 5 minutes away. I felt like I was out in the middle of nowhere and I might have had the wrong address until I saw this gate at the end of the street. I checked the GPS and it said to keep going straight. *Ace must live in this gated community*, I thought as I stopped in front of it. I needed a password to open them and of course I didn't have that. I parked on the road and called Neek; it went to voicemail. I called again and got the same response. *What the fuck?* I thought as I turned off my engine. I had come too far and was too close to not see Ace now. I left a voicemal, leaned my seat back and waited.

Neek called me back a half an hour later.

"Hello," I answered.

"What's going on?"

"Not much, I was just seeing if you knew the code to Ace's gate?"

"Oh, yeah. I forgot about the gate. I think I have it in my phone from when I went to visit. Hold on, let me check…Are you there already?" she asked.

"No," I lied. I didn't want her to know I was here because I wasn't looking for revenge on Ace, but to win him back.

"Then how did you know that you needed a code?" she questioned.

"I'm assuming because rich neighborhoods always need a code or something to enter," I said, trying to play it off.

"Unn huh…here's the code right here. Are you ready?"

"Yeah," I said putting my phone on speaker and pulling up my notes on my phone to write down the number.

"30267"

"30267," I repeated to make sure I had it right.

"Yeah."

"Alright, I'm going to give all of this to my cousin and I'll keep you posted."

"Alright" she said and hung up the phone.

I sat there looking at the code. This gate was the only thing between Ace and me right now and I had the ability to open it now. The only question was if I was ready for what's on the other side. I pulled up to the gate and entered the numbers Neek just gave me. It started to open and I could feel my breathing getting heavier. I don't know if I was nervous or scared. *Maybe I was doing the wrong thing,* I thought as I pulled through the gates, searching for the address. I found the one I was looking for and parked on the other side. *I wonder if he's in there.* I got out the car and walked across the street. I walked up to the door and knocked. I waited a few minutes and knocked again. No one was coming to the door. Maybe he wasn't home or this wasn't even his house. I walked back to my car and decided to wait for a minute to see if he came home.

I waited on the street for an hour before I saw a car pull up in the driveway. I leaned my seat all the way back so he couldn't see me and waited for him to get out the car. Ace got out the driver's side then Tia got out of the passenger's. I couldn't believe what I was seeing; these two muthafuckers looked like a happy family. I wanted to go over there and knock the fuck out of both of them, but I decided to play cool. *I'll get my revenge one way or the other*, I thought as I pulled out my phone. "Hello" I said when he answered.

"Hey Cuz, what's going on?"

"Not much over here, I was just seeing if you was still down to do me that favor?" I asked, watching them walk in the house.

"What favor?" he asked.

"The kind I can't talk about over the phone."

"Alright, when do you want to meet up?"

"In two days. I'm coming home and I'll see you then."

"You know where I'll be."

"I'll call you." I said and hung up the phone. At first I didn't want anything to happen to Ace, but it's clear that he's in love with Tia. I hated the fact that I lost him to a fucking child and they both were going to pay for playing with my emotions. *Ace for breaking my heart and Tia for stealing my man*, I thought as I started up the car and drove off. There was no use in sitting here getting madder. I had everything I needed and everybody would get theirs.

Tia

I'd been spending the last week with Ace and I was leaving today. I lay in bed looking at him. He was still sleeping and he looked so peaceful. I gave him a kiss on the cheek and headed for the bathroom.

I was getting ready to leave. Ace was stressed these last few days and I was glad I could be there to take some of it away. I knew I should hate him for what he did to me, but I still love him. It's something I couldn't explain.

"Where you going?" he asked when I came out the bathroom wrapped in a towel.

"You scared me!" I jumped.

"Where you going?" he asked again.

"I think it's time for me to go home," I said, turning toward him.

"I thought you were home."

"Now this is my home again?" I asked through chuckles.

"This has always been your home. Your key still works, doesn't it?"

"I don't know," I said, shrugging my shoulders. "I haven't used it."

"Come here."

I walked over to him. "What you want?" I said jokingly.

"You," he said, lifting up the covers.

"Now you want me again?" I said, cocking my head to the side.

"I've always wanted you, but I'm still trying to figure out how to overlook your betrayal."

"And I can't live with you loving me and hating me in the same breath," I said, turning around.

He grabbed my arm and pulled me back toward the bed.

"Come here." I climbed in the bed between his arms. "I missed you being here," he whispered in my ear.

"I miss you, too, but I can't live my life in fear anymore. I have somebody else to think about. I'm really sorry about Mike, but you have to get over it if you want to be with me."

"I'm trying, but it's not that easy," he said kissing me on the cheek.

"I know, I fucked up, but so did you and you have to accept that. Hell, I had to forgive you for hitting me, spitting in my face, and killing him. So I think you can get over one thing I've done."

"I'll try, but what you did was foul."

"And what you did wasn't?" I said looking at him funny. I pulled the covers back and was about to get up but he pulled me back down. "Let me get up."

"Naw," he said, sliding his hand under my towel.

"I don't feel like having sex," I said, moving his hand.

"Come on, baby," he said, kissing me on the neck.

"I can't. My stomach hurts. I need to get dressed anyways." I got off the bed and walked over to the closet.

"You still haven't told me where you were going."

"I told you. Home."

"Are you going to come back?"

"I'll come back to visit when I can."

"What the fuck you mean when you can?" he said, getting mad.

"Why are you getting upset?"

"You don't tell me, no, when you can."

"Well, what am I supposed to say? I don't know when I can come back, but when I can I will."

"And what are you doing in Michigan that's so important?"

"I'm registering for school and I don't know if you remember but I have to stop my best friend from putting my baby daddy in jail."

"Don't call me your fucking baby daddy."

"That's what you are, aren't you?"

"No, I'm your man and I better not hear about you giving my goods to anybody."

"You're not my man and that's the last thing on my mind," I said rolling my eyes. "That's all you think about."

"That's not all I think about, but I'd hate to have to kill another person."

"So are you going to kill everybody I'm with?"

"Nope because you're not going to be with anybody but me."

"If you say so."

Ace got up and walked over to me. "Don't play with me, Tia," he said, looking me in the eyes. "We've had a good week and I want to keep it like that."

I didn't say anything, but continued to put my clothes on. "Let's go to breakfast before I leave." I said trying to change the subject.

"Alright, let me get dressed," he said and walked away.

I got dressed and went downstairs to wait on Ace who came down about an hour later. He always took forever to get dressed. *I swear in some aspects he's like a girl.*

"You ready?" he asked.

"I've been ready, just waiting on you to get all dolled up," I laughed.

"Funny. Where do you want to eat?"

"Some place good," I said, getting off the couch. I walked toward the door and opened it. "I'm ready."

"You're awful bossy today," he said, walking toward me.

"It's the new me and we don't take any B.S.," I said, walking out the door. I made a vow to myself that even if I did get back with Ace that I wasn't going for that abusive ish anymore.

Katrice

I met up with Cheese and told him what I wanted done. The plans had changed and I wanted him to take Ace and Tia out. If I couldn't have him I didn't want anybody else too. I still wanted it to look like a carjacking, but now with two homicides. I gave him the address a couple of days ago and he assured me he would make it happen, but today I saw Tia on campus with Neek. "Hey guys," I said, walking up to them.

"Hey," Neek said. Tia didn't say anything; she just stood there staring at me.

"Hey, Tia," I said, addressing her personally.

"Hey," she said dryly.

"Do we have a problem? I know you probably know about Ace and me, but I'm not tripping over that."

"Me neither and why would I be? That's was before me."

"Exactly, so let's all just get along."

"Deal."

"Neek, do you still want me to do that?" I asked, referring to the Ace situation.

"Yeah."

"Alright, I already have my cousin on it. I'll let you know when it's done." I said and walked away. I had to think of a new plan to get Tia because she wasn't in Chicago, but Ace could still get it now.

Shynika

146

"What was that all about?" Tia asked when Katrice walked away.

"I wanted her to do something for me."

"What?"

"Nothing serious." I wanted to tell Tia what I was doing but I didn't know how she would take it, especially since she just came back from seeing him.

"So y'all friends now?" she asked, rolling her eyes.

"What? I can't have friends?"

"You can have friends, but it's not supposed to be with my enemies."

"I didn't know you had enemies," I joked.

"Whatever," she said and walked away.

"So you're mad now?" I yelled.

"Just disappointed." She turned around and said, "But don't worry about it. You can continue to do you," she said and started walking again.

Tia

I couldn't believe this bullshit, Neek and Katrice being friends. *Am I tripping or what?* I thought as I walked back to the apartment. I was on campus, registering for next semester, but I was thinking about moving back to Chicago and trying to make it work with Ace. I got back to the apartment and went in my room. I didn't feel like being bothered with anyone and I felt betrayed. Now I understand how Ace felt about Mike and me. I climbed in the bed to go to sleep. Ever since I got pregnant all I ever wanted to do was sleep and eat. I slept for a few hours, got up, and went to the bathroom. On my way I saw Neek sitting on the couch watching T.V. I didn't say anything because I was still kind of mad at her.

"Are you mad at me?" she asked me on my way back.

"More like hurt."

"Well, let's talk about it."

"Okay," I said, walking over to the couch. "I don't think it is right for you to be all cool with somebody that used to deal with my man. I wouldn't do that to you and I expect the same from my bestie."

"I can understand that and I'm sorry if I hurt your feelings, but we're not friends. I've been talking to her because she's helping me do something."

"What?"

"I can't tell you."

"So now we're keeping secrets from each other?" I said and got up.

"Where are you going?"

"To my room. I'm not going to talk to you if you're not going to tell me the truth."

"Okay, okay I'll be truthful" she said and took a deep breath.

I sat back down and looked at Neek. "Start talking."

"I don't know how you're going to take it so I'll just say it. I've been talking to Katrice because we're trying to make a plan to get rid of Ace."

"To get rid of who?" I asked in shock.

"Ace."

"Not my Ace?" I asked putting my hand on my chest.

"Yes, your Ace."

"And why would y'all do that?" I asked trying to keep my cool.

"Because he's no good and he needs to stop putting his hands on you."

"I know that's not why Katrice is involved."

"No, she's mad because he broke her heart."

"Wow!" I said trying to process what I just heard. "So let me get this right. My best friend is plotting with somebody else to kill my man?" I asked looking at her. She didn't say anything and that made me madder. "So now you're not talking?" I snapped.

"I don't know what to say. I thought I was doing the right thing by getting rid of him. Hell, he was beating the fuck out of you and I couldn't understand why you wouldn't leave."

"So, you were just going to kill him and make me leave?"

"Yeah."

"This is some crazy shit right here, like straight out of a movie. What made you get involved?"

"Since I came to stay with you for that week and found out he was putting his hands on you."

"That's been a few months. Damn, y'all been planning this a long time." I chuckled. "So, since we're being honest tell me the truth. Did you call the police on him too?"

"Yeah."

I looked at her and shook my head. "You're just trying to get rid of him by any means necessary," I said and got up. I couldn't sit right here anymore; she disgusted me. "I'm going to go and pack my clothes. I'm leaving," I said without facing her and started walking toward my room.

"Where are you going?"

"Someplace where I don't have to worry about being stabbed in the back. I know Ace has his flaws, but he's never lied to me and I know he loves me. If you had such a problem with it you should have come to me instead of going behind my back trying to solve the problem yourself...I can't believe you," I said walking in the room.

"I'm sorry," she said walking behind me.

"You're sorry? I bet you are, but not for what you did," I turned and looked at her. I walked over to her standing in the doorway and looked her straight in the face. "You're sorry because I found out. You still want Ace gone and I believe you'll do anything to make that happen," I said and slammed the door in her face. I finished packing my bags and headed out.

150

I stopped in front of the door and turned to face Neek who was sitting back on the couch. "So how were y'all going to do it? Since you're just so gangsta now," I asked.

"Katrice was going to get her cousin to do it. Tia, I'm really sorry," she said and started crying.

"Not as sorry as I am," I said. Grabbed my bag and walked out the door. I couldn't believe Neek would do that to me. She was the last person I would ever expect to stab me in the back. I've known her since I've had memories and we have so many of each other's secrets. I jumped in my car and dialed Ace's number. "What you doing?" I asked when he answered.

"Nothing."

"Guess what?"

"What Tia?"

"I guess Neek did call the police on you."

"I told you that."

"I know and you were right, but she's also plotting with your ex, Katrice, to take you out."

"What?"

"You heard me. They're trying to kill you!" I cried. "I can't believe it. I thought she was my best friend, but best friends wouldn't stab you in the back like that." I thought about what I was saying and who I was saying it to and I stopped. "But I guess I shouldn't be saying this to you. I'm sorry, you don't want to hear about that."

"You don't have to be sorry. I know exactly how you feel. Betrayal hurts."

"You're right. Now I understand why you did what you did and why you hate me so much."

"I don't hate you. It just hurts, but you have to learn to live with it or stop fucking with that person."

"Which one is it for us? I know the baby is why I'm still around, but have you forgiven me a little bit since you've had time to cool down?"

"Maybe a little but we have about four months to really know, but back to these bitches. How were those two planning on taking me out?" he asked through chuckles.

"Katrice's cousin is going to do it."

"You mean was. That bitch just doesn't learn. I've already told her it was nothing and she just seems to not want to get over it. I fucked her for a few months and she was addicted," he chuckled.

"I heard it was more like a year and y'all were dating."

"Yeah, closer to a year, but dating, no. I took her on a few dates but I had other females the whole time."

"Well, maybe you were just being a dog and she didn't know it."

"Oh, she knew it because I let it be known. Come on, Tia, you know me and you know I'm not

152

for any bullshit. Do I seem like the type of guy that would lead a girl on?"

I thought about what he said and he was right. He would have let her know exactly what it was and she could play the part or get to stepping. "No."

"She just couldn't handle the fact that she would never be my girl. Hell, she probably wants you out of the picture, especially if she knows you're pregnant."

"She knows," I said, rubbing my stomach.

"You better be careful, but I know why Katrice wants me dead so what's Neek excuse?"

"She doesn't like the fact that I won't leave you and you put the hands on me. But I told her not to worry about that because that wasn't happening anymore," I said, trying to diffuse her position. I was hurt by her right now, but I didn't want Ace to do anything to her either.

"I'm working on it. So when is this supposed to go down?"

"I don't know but I'm pretty sure it's soon."

"How did you find this out anyways?"

"I heard them talking and I confronted her, but why does that matter? You sound like you're not even concerned. I just said somebody was trying to kill you and you're extremely calm about it."

"Am I supposed to be scared? Well, I'm not. I can handle myself."

"I guess, but just be careful."

"You worried about me?"

"A little."

"Well, why don't you come watch my back?"

"I can't."

"Why not?"

"It's not right. Last week was good, but I know it won't be like that all the time."

"I can't promise it will, but I can promise that I'll work on it. I love you."

"But I betrayed you and you'll never trust me again. I wish I could come, but I know it's not the right thing to do. Watch your back and I love you," I said and hung up. I was going to go there, but I changed my mind. Neek was right about Ace not being good for me, but I didn't know what to do about my feelings. *I love that man and he's the first person I've ever been with and you know what they say about your first.* I pulled out the driveway and headed to a hotel. I couldn't deal with Neek right now. I checked into the room and cried myself to sleep. My life was so confusing and I didn't know what to do next.

Chapter 10
Tameka

It'd been two weeks since Ace was arrested. The prosecutor informed us that they had to drop the charges due to not having enough evidence, but they were sure he did it. I asked them why they were so sure and they informed us about the hotel incident. Apparently Mike and Tia were having sex for a while at this one hotel and Ace found out and snapped. I couldn't believe this was going on, but it was all starting to make sense. Mike's body wasn't found and they didn't have anything, but her say as evidence which wasn't enough. I believed the prosecutor because Ace hadn't made any contact with us after his arrest and he didn't seem to be concerned about Mike's disappearance. I was pissed. Ace had murdered Mike and was about to get away with it. I was mad about the affair, but Mike didn't deserve to die. I was sitting on the couch crying my eyes out. There was no way Ace was going to get away with this. *I'm going to get revenge for Mike's death if it's the last thing I do,* I thought as I rolled a blunt. *I never really liked Ace to begin. He has always thought he could do whatever he wanted, but he was going to learn today.*

I started thinking of ways to pay him back. Maybe I could kill him myself, but I knew I couldn't do that. I didn't have the heart to kill someone, but that didn't mean I couldn't hire someone. I called a few of my people and they put me in contact with this girl; they said she was the best person for the job if I wanted it done right and quick. *I am meeting up with her today,* I thought as I walked in the restaurant not sure who I was looking for. All I knew was she was wearing all black with a yellow tie. I walked to the back of the restaurant and took a seat. A few minutes later a short lady walked up in all black. I really couldn't see her face, but I could see the yellow tie and I knew it was her. She sat across from me never taking off her hat. "Did you bring the information?" she asked, getting straight to the point.

"It's right here," I said, pulling out the envelope. I slid it across the table to her, giving her all the information I had on Ace.

"I'll be in touch," she said and started to get up.

"Wait, I didn't even get your name and I had some more questions."

"The less you know the better. You don't need to ask questions. I'll be in touch and you can call me Sky," she said and walked away.

The ball was in motion and it was only a matter of time before Ace get what was coming to him. I paid for my drink and left with no regrets. I didn't know how I would feel about ordering a hit, but all I had to do was think about him killing Mike and I knew I had to make him pay.

Sky

I pulled up to my loft downtown, grabbed the envelope, and headed to the elevator. My loft was on the 15th floor and I'd be damned if I walked all those stairs. I opened the door, threw the envelope on the end table, and went to take a shower. I took a nice long shower then went to sleep. I had been working for two days straight to get my last mark and I needed some rest. *I'll look at that later*, I thought as I closed my eyes and fell asleep.

I woke up and looked at the time; it was 1 in the afternoon. I had slept all day. "Damn, I must have been tired," I said out loud. I lay there for a few more minute and then went to freshen up. I sat on the bed, turned on the TV, and was about to get comfortable when I remembered I had that envelope in there. I got off the bed, grabbed it and went back in my room. I dumped the contents of the envelope on the bed and proceeded to look through them when I recognized the face. This was the same guy who was hitting on me a few weeks ago when I was doing another job.

I thought back to that day; this wife let me know where to find her cheating husband and paid me to kill him. I put on one of my freakem dresses and got prepared to freak the life out of my next victim, literally. I met up with his wife earlier that day and she informed me that he was going to be at Primary. I made my way to the club. There was a line but I'd be damned if I waited. I walked up to the bouncer. "Hey Sky," he said as I approached. I had made a lot of connections over the years and done enough favors to be alright in this world. Which also meant that I definitely wasn't waiting in anyone's line.

"What's up?"

"Same ol', same ol'. How've you been?"

"You know I'm always good," I answered and walked through the door. I told a few of my girls to meet me up here for some drinks. Nobody really knew what I did but a handful of people so you had to know somebody in my world to get to me. I walked around the club until I found my target sitting in the VIP booth. He was surrounded by females and pouring everybody's drinks. I spotted my girls by the bar next and headed over to them. "Damn, y'all didn't even wait on me," I said, walking up behind them.

"Who knew when you were really going to get here? You're always late," my friend Brook said.

I looked at my phone. "I'm only 30 minutes late."

"This time."

We have been friends for a few years and were really close, well as close as I could get to someone considering what I do. Nobody knew my real life and what I really did; they only knew what I showed them. "I'm working on that, see? I'm getting better." I laughed.

"You are," she said, sipping her drink.

"Y'all didn't get me a drink?" I said, getting the bartender's attention.

"What can I get you?"

"A Blue Motorcycle."

"Here you go" he said handing me my drink. I tipped him a few dollars, grabbed some napkins, and turned back to my circle. "Let's go to the dance floor." I was in the middle of a conversation with Brook when I felt somebody staring at me. We locked eyes for a minute and I turned away, and then the next thing I know he was standing behind me asking can he buy me a drink. I looked back at the picture. He said his name was Anthony Ealy, and I can't lie the man was handsome. *Talk about a small world, this is going to be this easiest mark I've ever hit,* I thought, thinking about my plan to get this job done. *I know he's already feeling me so all I have to do is run into him somewhere and I know I got him from there.* I read through his file and he was the NFL player that was charged with murder a couple of weeks ago. Who would have even known? I thought, putting down the file and walking in the kitchen.

Shynika

I had to tell Tia everything; she knew something was up when Katrice came up talking to me. I was hoping that she would be with me and we could all plan this together, but I should have known better. She loved that man and would do anything for him, after all he was her first. I called Katrice. "Hello," I said when she answered.

"What's going on?"

"I told Tia."

"You told Tia what?"

"About our plan to get rid of Ace."

"And why did you do that? You know she's going to tell Ace."

"I know, I know. That's why I think we should call the whole thing off."

"Call the whole thing off? No, I'm not doing that."

"And why not?"

"Because if Ace knows then I'm dead and so are you. Plus I already have my cousin on the job."

"Well, you can call your cousin and call it off. I don't want to go through with this anymore. He is my best friend's baby daddy and it will kill her if he's dead."

"You think I give a fuck about her?" she yelled. "She's the reason I'm not with him now."

"Don't blame Tia for that. If that was your man then she wouldn't have been able to come and

160

snatch him like that. Obviously it wasn't what you thought it was and you were living a fantasy," I snapped.

"Whatever, I don't care what you say. I'm not calling shit off," she said and hung up the phone.

I picked up the phone and tried to call Tia, but it went straight to voicemail. I left her a message explaining how sorry I was and hung up. I called back a few more times and sent a few text messages, but I didn't get any responses. I had fucked up and somehow I had to make this right. I had to stop Katrice from going through with her plan, but I didn't know who her cousin was and there was no way she was going to tell me now.

Katrice

I couldn't believe that little bitch had told Tia about our plan. I knew Tia told Ace and now everything was fucked up. Ace was going to be expecting us and he's not going to get caught off guard. I called Cheese on the phone.

"What's up, Cuz?"

"A lot. Ace knows about our plan."

"How does he know?"

"The girl I got the address from told him and now he's going to be expecting us."

"What do you want to do about it?"

"I still wanna go through with it."

"Are you sure? He's going to know it's you and what if he tells someone before it happens? Or what if the other girl tells? This is risky right now."

"So you don't wanna do it?"

"Maybe we should wait until things cool down."

"Wait until things cool down? And when would that be? No, we need to do it right now. What you scared of?"

"Getting caught."

"And how is that going to happened?"

"If I get caught or Ace comes up missing right now, you're going to be the first suspect."

"No, he just got arrested for killing Mike so they're going to think it's someone who wants revenge."

"I still say we should wait. I'll watch things for a few days and let you know when I think it's time. I'm still going to do it. I just want to make sure we're smart about it."

"Alright," I said and hung up the phone. *I hate Tia even more*, I thought. *She is always fucking up my plans. I can't wait until the day she gets what's coming to her.*

Tia

I woke the next morning, took a shower, and turned my phone on. I had a few messages from Neek. I didn't know why she was calling me. I thought I made it very clear that I wasn't fucking with her. I listened to the first message and it was her on there, crying about how sorry she was. I rolled my eyes and deleted all the messages. I didn't want to deal with her and I don't know how long I need to get over this or if I'll ever get over this. I put on some clothes and headed out the door. I needed some time away from everything. I was close to 5 months pregnant and I needed to start worrying about my baby and stop stressing about all this other shit. I got in my car and headed home.

I drove back to my mom's house in Kalamazoo. I walked in the house and my mom was sitting in the living room watching TV.

"Hey Mom," I said and closed the door.

"Hey, baby, what you doing here?"

"I needed to get away from my life. Everything is wrong and I don't know how to fix it!" I cried.

"Come here, baby," she said, holding her arms out.

I walked over to my mom and put my head on her chest and cried. I wanted to tell my mom everything, but I didn't know if I should.

"What's wrong, baby?" she said, rubbing my head.

"I don't know where to start. So much has been going on this last year."

"Like what?" she asked.

"Well to start, Ace has been abusive."

"What?" she said and pulled away from me. She lifted my face and looked me in the eyes "Ace has been what?"

"Abusive," I said and lowered my eyes. I hadn't told my mom anything because she was always at work. My mom worked a lot of hours to make sure I had the best life and I was too ashamed to tell her that I was getting knocked upside my head instead of focusing on school.

"How long?"

"Since I moved to Chicago."

"Why haven't you told me? I would have been there for you."

"I didn't want to disappoint you and I was ashamed."

"That wouldn't have disappointed me. Not telling me is what disappoints me."

"I'm sorry. I just didn't know how to tell anybody."

"Nobody knew?"

"Neek and Marcus just found out."

"Marcus knew?"

"Yeah, he came and got me a couple of weeks ago."

"And that's his baby?"

"Yes, Mom," I said and started crying. "I wanted to leave, but I couldn't. I don't know what's wrong with me. Why do I still love him after everything he's done to me?"

"Baby, that's not your fault. We all do some foolish things for love; it's just something nobody can explain. The good thing is you're out of it and I'm here for you and the baby. Everything is going to be alright," she said, kissing me on the forehead.

"I don't know about that. Neek is trying to kill Ace now."

"Why is she trying to do that?"

"Because she wants me to leave him."

"But you're not with him anymore."

"I know, but I saw him last week and now she thinks I'll go back."

"I wouldn't even worry about that. Neek doesn't have it in her to kill someone. Ace seems like he can take care of himself anyways. I know you still love him, but it will get easier over time."

I lay there in my mom's arms for a few more minutes before I got up and walked toward my room. "I need some rest," I said looking at her. "I'll see you tomorrow."

"Are you going to be here tomorrow?" she asked

"Yeah, why did you ask me that?"

"Because last time you said that I came home from work and you were gone."

"I'll be here this time" I said walking to my room.

I climbed in my bed and passed out. I was drained. I woke up the next morning and made me a doctor's appointment. I had one next week for my five months checkup in Ann Arbor and since I wasn't going to be there I made one with my doctor here. Despite everything going on in my life I still made sure my baby was taken care of. Plus I was finding out the sex of my baby and I was excited about it. I also started looking for places to stay; I needed to get more stable and get my life together. I made a list of two bedrooms I was interested in and started calling around. I set up a few appointments to view them and walked out of my room. I went to the living room and nobody was there. I peeked in my mom's room and it was empty. *Where did she go?* I thought as I walked in the kitchen. I was hungry and needed some food. I went to my room, threw on some clothes, and headed out to get me some food.

I went to this fish shack on the eastside and ordered me some Tilapia. Tilapia was my favorite fish and this place had the best. I got that along with some fries then went back home. I sat on the couch, ate my food and watched a few of my favorite shows. I was bored and needed to get out of the house, so I decided to do a little shopping and get my nails done. I pulled up to the nail shop and it wasn't too busy.

"Can I help you?" a Chinese woman asked when I walked in.

"I want a pedicure and full set," I said holding up my nails. I hadn't had my nails done in months and I was well overdue.

"You can have a seat and we'll be right with you," she said, pointing to the chairs to my right. I sat down and waited until it was my turn.

Ace

It had been two weeks since Tia had told me somebody was trying to kill me. I was also officially cut from Chicago. My life had changed in a blink of an eye and I didn't know where to go from here. All my endorsements were also gone. I was just thankful I was smart enough to invest my money instead of blowing it all so I would still have a paycheck and be able to maintain my lifestyle. I was also starting to find out who my real friends were. I had gotten a few calls from Mike's mom, but I couldn't face her. Dawn was like a mom to me and she would know if I was lying or not; I knew one day I was going to come face to face with her, but not today. They declared my brother dead and had a funeral without a body; I didn't attended but I sat outside the church and held my own service. I also followed them to the grave site and shed on last tear for my brother. I took a sip of my Ciroc and thought back to the good days when Mike and I were inseparable.

I thought about the day we both got accepted to U of M and how much fun the first three years were. We were the stars on campus and had everything at our fingertips. We partied every weekend and got any girl we wanted. I remembered a lot of drinking, smoking, laughing, and partying. I sat back on the couch, thinking about my brother and for the first time I regretted what I did. I was angry and shouldn't have made a decision like that until I had calmed down. Now my brother was gone and I couldn't blame anybody but myself. I should have never let a female come between us. My phone started to ring and it was Brian; he was the only person I had really been talking too lately.

"What's up?"

"I can't call it. What you doing tonight, bro?"

"Nothing, why?"

"My girl has this friend and they want to go to the comedy show tonight, but her date cancelled."

"And you need me to come? Now you know I don't do blind dates."

"I know, but shorty is bad and I wouldn't send you on some bullshit."

"I don't really feel like being bothered."

"Come on, Ace. You need to get out the house anyways."

He was right, I did need to get out the house but I didn't want to go on a date in the process. "You're right," I said giving in. "But she better be bad."

"Oh she is, if she wasn't my girl's friend I would hit her."

"Nigga, you hit everybody," I said and started laughing.

"Whatever, nigga, just be ready at 8."

"Alright, but I'll meet y'all there," I said and hung up the phone. I got off the couch and headed upstairs. I went in the bathroom and turned on the shower I went to the closet, found me something to wear, and lay it on the bed. I got in the shower, shaved, and walked out of the room. I was glad it was a comedy show because I needed a good laugh.

I rolled a few blunts and put on a three piece black suit with a white shirt. I threw on my white and white shoes and headed out the door. It was after 8. I jumped in my car and headed toward the theater. I got there at 8:45, valeted my car, and called Brian.

"Where you at?"

"I'm here, where you at?"

"We're sitting toward the front at one of the tables." The where seats like and auditorium for most of the seating, but the VIP tables were at the front where they were sitting. I walked in and it was packed. I walked to the front and saw Mike sitting at a table by the stage. I walked over to him and sat down. Brian was the only one at the table.

"Did I take too long?" I asked Brian as I looked around the table.

"Naw! They had to go to the restroom. They should be right back," he said.

I pulled out the chair that didn't have a drink in front of it and sat down. I started checking my surroundings and there were some fine woman in here tonight. *If my date wasn't bad then I wouldn't have any problem replacing her,* I thought.

"How do y'all know this girl?" I asked a little curious.

"Mya and she met at the gym and they've been hanging out for a few weeks now. She was the one who got the tickets, but her date bailed on her. She wanted us to just call another couple, but I called you instead. It would have been fucked up to not take her, after all she's the one who gave us the tickets."

"Why did she get stood up?"

"Now you know I don't know all of that. I only know the other stuff because Mya kept going on and on about how wrong it would be to go without her and how I needed to call one of my friends and all that other shit."

"Yeah, I know how that it." I said as the waitress came over.

"Can I get you anything?" she asked, holding out her pad and pen.

"I'll take a beer."

"Okay, I'll be right back" she said and walked away.

A few minutes later the girls came walking back to the table and the shorty Mya was walking with was bad. She was short, chocolate, and had long curly hair which I'm sure was fake. Her body was petite but sexy. She had on a jumpsuit and I could see all her curves and she had a handful of everything.

170

When she got closer she started to look familiar, but I couldn't place her. *I am probably tripping*, I thought as they reached the table.

"Hey guys," Mya said as they reached the table.

"Hey," we both said.

"I'm glad to see you finally made it," she said, looking at me.

"I told y'all I was coming."

"Better late than never, but this is my friend, Sky. Sky this is Ace," she said, introducing us. *Sky, that named sounded real familiar*, and then it hit me. Sky was the girl I met at the club that night. *What a small world,* I thought as I sat there with a smile on my face, thinking how my luck was finally turning around.

Sky

I leaned over and whispered in his ear, "You look real familiar," knowing exactly where I knew him from.

"You look like a woman I tried to buy a drink for at the club a few weeks ago," he said as the waitress approached with his drink.

"Tell me a little about this woman?" I said, flirting with him; he was handsome.

"She was beautiful, but I really didn't get a chance to know her because she had a little attitude."

"I didn't have an attitude! I already had a drink" I laughed.

"Oh, so you do remember me?"

"How could I forget?" I giggled.

"Shh, we're trying to listen to the show," Mya whispered.

"Well excuse me," I whispered back and smiled at Ace.

"We'll talk later," he whispered in my ear.

I smiled to myself because I knew I had him. *This was going to be easier than I could have dreamed,* I thought as I turned and watched the show.

Katrice

A few weeks had gone by since I'd talked to Neek. Tia hadn't been on campus since Neek told me she told her and I wasn't talking to her to ask her why. *I bet she went back to Chicago with Ace.* I hated the thought of them being together. *Bitch, you don't leave me for no kid,* I thought as I called my cousin.

"What's up, Cuz?"

"Nothing, you ready to finish this thing?"

"I'm already on it."

"What do you mean you're already on it?" I asked in shock.

"I've been here on the job for the past week."

"And what's been going on?" I asked, trying to figure out what Ace has been up to.

"Nothing really. He's just been running around with some girl these last two weeks."

"What girl?" I asked curious.

172

"I don't know. My job is not to figure out who he's fucking."

"What does she look like? Is she short?" I asked annoyed.

"Yeah but not too short. She's thick, chocolate, and bad. I'll fuck her."

"I guess, is she pregnant?"

"Naw, shorty aint pregnant."

She wasn't pregnant so the girl couldn't be Tia. *Who is Ace shacking up with now*? I thought still on the phone.

"I'll call you back later," he said and hung up.

I hung up the phone mad as hell. What was the point of taking Tia out if Ace was just going to move on to the next girl that still wasn't me? I guess I could give her a pass, but Ace still had to go. I couldn't stand to see him happy and I wanted him to pay for what he did to me.

Sky

I'd been spending the last two weeks with Ace and I was really enjoying myself, but that wasn't going to stop me from doing what I came here to do. *I got a job and I am waiting on the right time,* I thought as I lay next to him. He was different and if I would have gotten to know him under different circumstances I probably would have feelings for him, which is something I would never do. I got off the bed and put my clothes on. I needed to stop spending the night here because that's how people get caught up. I needed to hurry up and get this job done and I promised myself I'd do it by the end of the week. I snuck out his room and headed to my car. I needed to stay away from him for a few days so I could get my mind right. I drove to my loft, lay in my bed, and went back to sleep within five minutes.

I woke the next morning to my phone ringing.

"Hello," I said without looking at the name.

"Hey Sky, why did you sneak out on my like that?" I heard Ace ask.

"I had an emergency and I needed to leave."

"Is everything alright?"

"Yeah, now it is."

"What happened?"

"Nothing really and I'll rather not talk about it," I said, lying because there was nothing to talk about.

"Alright, I hope everything is alright. Am I going to see you later?"

"Naw, I had to go out of town to see my parents. I'll be back in a few days," I lied again.

"Alright, I'll see you then." He said and hung up.

I needed to map out my plan and being under him all the time was not the way to do it. I threw the phone on the bed and went back to sleep.

Cheese

I had been watching this nigga for over a week now and he was spending a lot of time with this chick. "This job might be harder than I thought," I said out loud to myself. I was sitting outside of his house when I saw her sneaking out. *Where was she going?* I thought as she sped out the driveway. I was thinking about sneaking in Ace's house and doing the job right now, but I didn't know if shorty was coming back or not so I decided to chill. I sat out there until the sun rose and she never came back. I watched his spot all morning and there was nothing going on. At about 1 he came out and jumped in the car. I started my car and followed him downtown to this restaurant. This shit was getting boring as fuck and I was ready to get this job done and over with.

I watched Ace for a few more days and shorty wasn't around anymore. They must have gotten into a fight? *Now was my time to strike,* I thought watching him walk into the barber shop. I left to get some food because I knew it was going to take a few for him to get cut so I went down the street to this soul food joint. I got my food and parked back in my spot. I could see Ace sitting in the chair. I lent my chair back and went in on the ribs I ordered. I ate all my food and as I was wiping my hands when I looked up and seen Ace walking to his car. He jumped in and headed down the road with me following behind him. He went in to this restaurant and made a few more spots before heading home. He walked in the house and now was the time.

It was dark outside and I waited a few minutes before I got out the car. I walked up to the door and it was locked. I picked the lock, pulled my gun out, and crept into the house. The house was dark and there was nobody down stairs. I crept up the stairs. I looked around for somebody but I didn't see a soul. I could see a light coming from the bottom of the door and I knew this was it, this was his room. I put my ear to the door and I could hear the TV. I took a deep breath, griped my gun and got prepared for what was on the other side of the door. I opened the door slowly and let my gun go first, but to my surprise there was nobody there. I walked around the room and nobody. *Where's the nigga at?* I thought then heard the shower running behind another closed door. *This nigga is in the shower.* I opened the door and saw him standing in the shower. He was washing his hair and had his eyes closed. I walked up to the shower, opened the door and shot him two times in the chest. He opened his eyes and I heard him yell something, but I ran out the house, jumped in my car and sped off. I got back to my hotel and called Katrice.

Katrice

I woke up to my phone ringing. It was my cousin, Cheese. *I hope nothing happened to him,* I thought answering the phone. "Hello?"

"It's done," I heard him say. At first I was confused, and then it came to me.

"Are you serious?" I said in shock.

"Yeah, you should see it on the news tomorrow," he was short.

"Alright," I said a little excited.

"I gotta go," he said, hanging up.

I can't believe it was finally done, I thought, hanging up the phone. I had waited for this day for so long and I was happy about it, but I was sad, too. I didn't want anyone to have Ace, but now I was sad he was gone also. *Have I just made the worst decision of my life all because a man didn't want to be with me?* I thought as I closed my ears and cried silently.

Sky

A few days had gone by and I hadn't seen Ace, but today we had a date. I had called him and asked if I could take him out and of course he agreed. I was picking him up tonight and taking him to eat his last meal. He said he needed to run a few errands, but I can pick him up tonight. I took my time getting ready because I was falling for him and I wanted this last night to be special. I went to the mall and I got this long black dress that had the back out and a v-neck in the front. It was sexy, but classy and that was exactly what I was looking for. I picked some silver heels along with silver accessories. I went and got my hair curled and pinned up and headed home to get dressed. I took a long bubble bath and took my time on my makeup. I got dressed, did a once over and in the mirror, and I was looking nice. I grabbed my clutch and headed out the door to pick up my date.

I was almost to Ace's house when this car came flying past me and almost ran me off the road. "Slow the fuck down!" I yelled out the window and continued driving. I pulled up to the gate and entered the code he gave to me so I could come and go as I pleased. I pulled up to his house and the door was opened wide. I walked in the house yelling his name. "Ace!" I yelled and didn't get any response. I walked up the stairs to his room continuing to yell his name the whole time. I heard the shower running and I walked in the bathroom. I could see Ace's arm hanging out the shower. I ran over there and I saw him lying on the floor, holding his chest and there was blood running down the drain. "Oh my God" I screamed and pulled out my phone. I leaned down and put his head on my lap and called 911.

"911, what's your emergency?"

"My boyfriend was shot!" I yelled in the phone. I knew I was going to kill him tonight, but seeing him lying there did something to me and all I wanted to do was save him. I believed everything happens for a reason and there was a reason I walked into this house and saw him like this.

"Can you tell me what happened?"

"I don't know, I just walked into his house and found him like this. Please get someone here quick!" I said crying hysterically.

"Do you know the address?" she asked.

I looked through my text messages and gave them the address. Ace had texted it to me a few weeks back and I put it in my favorites.

"I'll send someone right over," she said.

I looked down at Ace and he was still alive. "It's alright, you're going to be alright," I said, rocking him in my lap and putting pressure on his wound. "Help is on the way," I said, rubbing his face. "Hello! Are they coming?"

"Yes, ma'am, someone is on their way."

I sat there holding Ace for what felt like forever before I heard sirens, I looked down at Ace and he was still breathing which was all I cared about. I had killed a few people and never thought twice about it, but being on this side of it made me want to change. If Ace made it out of this I was going to settle down and give this a try. *But if he doesn't I will kill any and everybody that was involved in this,* I thought as I felt someone grab my arm.

"Can you please step away ma'am?" I heard the paramedic say. One of them grabbed Ace's head off my lab and I stood up and stood to the side and started praying.

Also From NCM Publishing

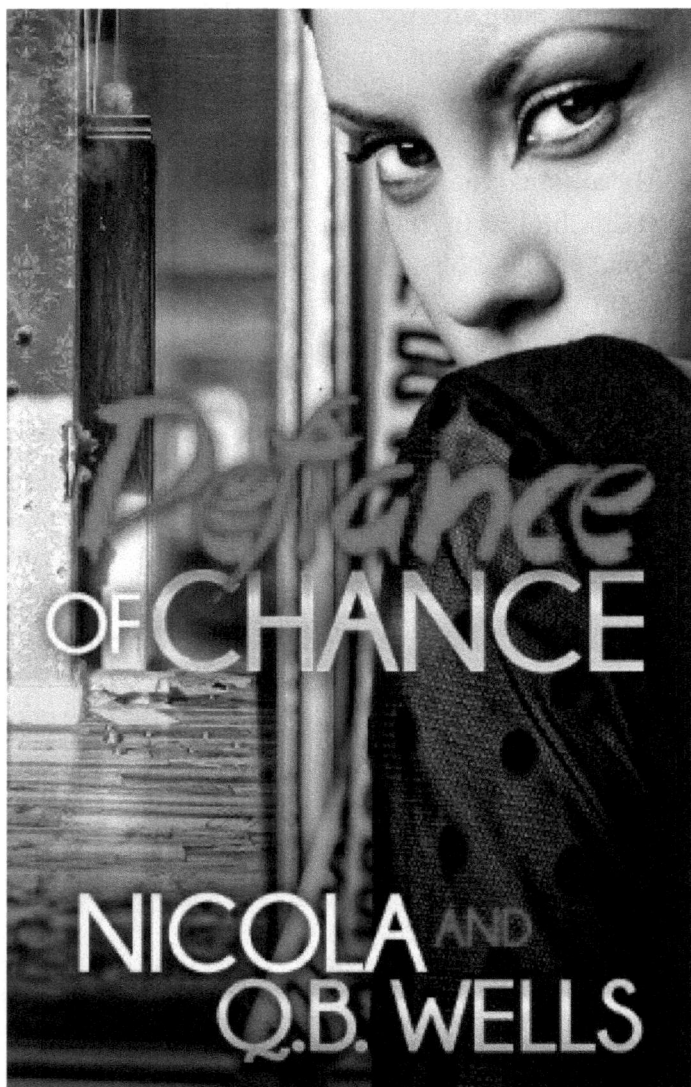

OF CHANCE

NICOLA AND Q.B. WELLS

Keyanna Ford

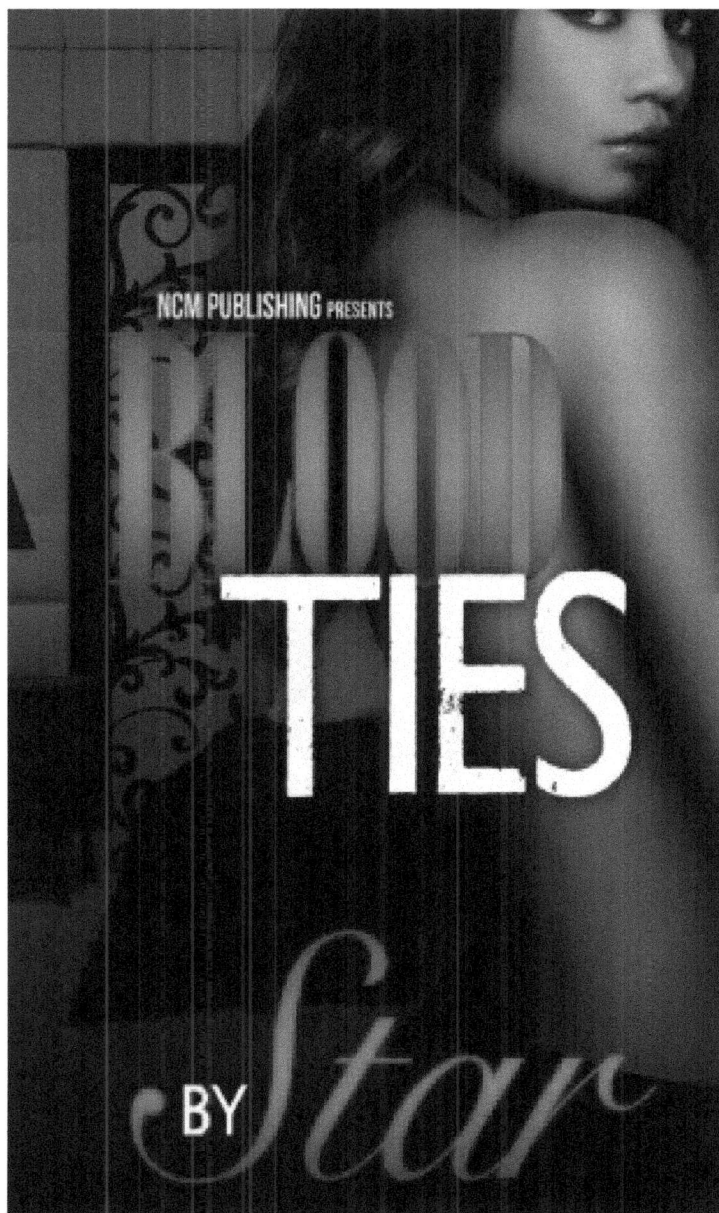

NCM PUBLISHING PRESENTS

BLOOD
TIES

BY *Star*

www.ingramcontent.com/pod-product-compliance
Lightning Source LLC
Chambersburg PA
CBHW051831090426
42736CB00011B/1741